MW00991596

Spirits

Dr. Gloria
Johnson-Rodgers

SPIRITS by Dr. Gloria Johnson-Rodgers
Published by Creation House
A Strang Company
600 Rinehart Road
Lake Mary, Florida 32746
www.creationhouse.com

Unless otherwise noted, all Scripture quotations are from the King James Version of the Bible.

Scripture quotations marked NKJV are from the New King James Version of the Bible. Copyright © 1979, 1980, 1982 by Thomas Nelson, Inc., publishers. Used by permission.

Scripture quotations marked AMP are from the Amplified Bible. Old Testament copyright © 1965, 1987 by the Zondervan Corporation. The Amplified New Testament copyright © 1954, 1958, 1987 by the Lockman Foundation. Used by permission.

Word definitions are derived from Margery Berube, ed., *Webster's II Collegiate Dictionary* (Boston, MA: Houghton Mifflin Company, 1995).

Design Director: Bill Johnson
Cover design by Jerry Pomales

Library of Congress Control Number: 2008932498
International Standard Book Number: 978-1-59979-398-6

First Edition

09 10 11 12 — 987654321
Printed in the United States of America

CONTENTS

Foreword vii

Introduction 1

Part I: Life in the Spirit World

1 The Ministry of Angels 9

2 The Work of Evil Spirits 29

3 Warfare in High Places 41

Part II: Spirits in the Enemy's Employ

4 Lust 57

5 Idolatry and Witchcraft 71

6 Negativity, Hatred, and Bitterness 85

7 Variance, Wrath, Strife, Sedition, and Heresies 95

8 Emulations, Envyings, and Murders 105

9 Offenses 113

10 Abuse 123

11 Stress 133

12 Generational Curses 147

13 Death 155

Part III: Healing for Spiritual Brokenness

14 Our Covenant Relationship With God 169

15 Healing Truth for Broken Marriages 181
16 Receiving Healing Through Release 195

Part IV: Blessed with All Spiritual Blessings

17 The Bottom Line 205
18 Full Deliverance 213
19 Our Walk with God 223
20 A Man After God's Own Heart 237
21 The Fruit of Fasting 247
Appendix A: A Supplement on Stress 255
Appendix B: Anorexia Nervosa, Bulimia, and Overeating 261
Appendix C: A Teenager's Thoughts on Prejudice and Stress 265
About the Author 273
Bibliography 277
Notes 283
To Contact the Author 287

FOREWORD

THROUGHOUT MY LIFE, I have had numerous encounters with spirits, but it wasn't until few years ago that I really began to understand them. I remember often asking "Auntie," my name for Dr. Gloria Johnson-Rodgers, about how spirits work and what effect they have on people and their actions. One day, as she was describing the first book she was working on, I suggested that she write a book on spirits, hoping that it would help countless people.

I believed then, and still believe now, that if we truly understand spirits and the capacities in which they operate, we will strive harder to govern our lives according to the Word of God, simply, if for no other reason, to avoid negative consequences. As 1 Samuel 15:22 says, "Behold, to obey is better than sacrifice." One of the greatest things about trying to improve our lives in our Christian walk is that we can have a ripple effect on the lives of other people, and the impact can be phenomenal. Imagine what the world would be like if everybody did and knew how to do "their part" in the body of Christ. Isn't now the perfect time to develop a greater understanding of spirits and gain a closer relationship to God?

My first year of college has been an eye-opening experience for me in all aspects of life and especially in the spiritual world. I have been surrounded by a diverse group of people with different backgrounds and beliefs, and I have witnessed spirits in some of their most extreme capacities. A lot of positive sharing has occurred, and at the same time, spiritual warfare has constantly been taking place.

During this time I have witnessed the consequences of a child being brought up under the guidance and love of God and a God-loving family versus the negative effects of generational curses, abuse, neglect, anger, and hatred, things that many of the girls on my hall have suffered. It has been reinforced in my mind, that the enemy always tries to block blessings when people are trying to move to "another level," the exact thing that every college student is in someway trying to do. In the midst of this battle, the greatest rewards of a college institution—establishing a greater love of the academic world, for one's fellow man, personal development, and more importantly, spiritual development—can sometimes be overshadowed by the plot of the devil. Because these girls had suffered abuse, they were unable to release past hurts and move forward.

I have also learned to embrace the scriptures "For he shall give his angels charge over thee, to keep thee in all thy ways" (Ps. 91:11), and "In all thy ways acknowledge him, and he shall direct thy paths" (Prov. 3:6). In all of this, I have grown to be truly happy to have a relationship with God, thankful for the encouraging people and messengers that He has sent in to my life, and appreciative to have some level of understanding about various spirits before encountering them. The Lord has definitely kept me!

A few months ago, three friends and I walked over to a neighboring college's library to study for exams. We went upstairs, sat down at a table, and began reading. When we took a break, we began talking about spiritual matters and discussed miracles we had witnessed and negative spirits we had noticed on campus.

About thirty minutes after we began talking, a man, probably in his fifties or sixties, stopped to talk to us. I guess he noticed that we had been talking about spiritual matters. He told us, "Do not fight against people who try to find fault with the Word of God by using carnal, scholastic knowledge, for the word of God is more advanced than any intellect." He later stated that the spirits we were dealing with in college were unlike the spirits we had dealt with before; they were stronger and required a different kind of prayer.

After he finished talking, he left us sitting in amazement. Who was this man and how did he know everything we had been experiencing? We had not talked about many of the things that he brought up. We knew he had to have a spiritual connection with God.

We went back to studying and agreed that we would leave to return to our campus around 11:30 p.m. A few minutes before we left, the man came back and began talking to us again. There had been much division between Christians of different denominations on campus, and without us even mentioning it, the man said, "Denominations are a creation of man and not God; this is why they often fail." Speaking personally into our lives, he explained that the Word of God was and is the most important thing in our spiritual walk.

I was again amazed as I tried to look into the fairly dark-brown man's blue eyes, which were strangely blinding. Then, at exactly 11:30 p.m., he looked at his watch and immediately left. My friends and I were speechless. It seemed as if the man knew everything about us. And what was even more peculiar, in the all the times we had gone to the library before, we had never seen him. We never saw him again.

—Tianna Johnson

INTRODUCTION

I HAD BEEN SLEEPING since about 10:00 p.m., but at 3:00 a.m., I awoke to see a beautiful creature above my head. I call her a creature, but she looked like a lady, suspended in mid-air over my bed. Her lovely face radiated the very essence of love, protection, peace, and goodwill, and she had long, thick, naturally curly, flowing blonde hair. Her long gown seemed endless. I saw no hands or feet.

The creature's smile was wide, but I saw no teeth because she did not open her mouth. She was altogether gentle, even adoring and caring, and she put me totally at ease. She literally said that all is well and would be well forever and ever. She was very calming and serene and promoted peace that surpasses all understanding. Her eyes were a beautiful light brown and saw all and knew all without a word being uttered. They said everything, all at the same time, and were fixed on me as I slept and even as I awoke. They seemed to speak to me, "Know that I see all, know that I am always here, and know that I will always be here for you."

Her creamy white skin was so smooth and soft that words cannot adequately describe it. It appeared to be even smoother than a newborn baby's behind. It was not pale at all, but so full of life and beauty, without age, stress, or worry. It had no wrinkles or hint of any spot or blemish and was free of any discoloration. Nothing that would suggest imperfection on any level existed.

The creature's beautiful blonde hair was waving in the air as if it were a beautiful spring day with gentle breezes that blew it just outward from her face. She had a full, thick head of hair that was straightened by her atmosphere. She appeared to be in a separate world with a different climate and elements that were vastly different than the one I was in. Yet she was in the same room.

Her gown appeared to be of the finest satin or silk. The material was so thin and elegant that you could almost see through it, but it was not transparent. It was simply a continuous flow of something indescribably beautiful. There was no wrinkle in the cloth, no imperfection, but a constant flow of finery. The color was the purest white, with no comparison to anything one could see in a fabric shop or among clothes produced by the most exquisite tailor.

One moment the creature was there, and in the twinkling of an eye she faded into the air. She faded as if she had not left the physical spot but only my vision of viewing; she was not gone, but I was not to see her all the time. I knew in my heart that I was her assignment, and a great and wonderful sense of security came over me. No fear or despair or doubt entered into my mind. I was not asleep or dreaming.

Ten years later, the morning after a very traumatic experience, I awoke to find the remnants of the creature's garments disappearing yet remaining in place as I opened my eyes in a different room and even a different house. I had drifted off to sleep the night before, praying and searching and asking, Why me? The assurance of her presence was there as I awoke. It was plain to see that she was and is definitely watching over me at all times even when I sleep.

Who or what was this creature, and what was she doing? The *who* of the matter is the question at hand. Obviously she was not human or of this world but what most would call a spirit.

The Beginning of Spiritual Conflict

This is a book about spirits, both good and evil. *Webster's Collegiate Dictionary* defines a spirit as "a supernatural being or essence, a malevolent being that enters and possesses a human being, an often malevolent being that is bodiless but can become visible." It recognizes that spirits exist and that they can appear and then become invisible. There are many accounts of spirits, ghosts, angels, or even devils, and they may or may not be true. I can only speak for what I have seen.

According to the Bible, the entire host of angels was at one time considered good and worshiped God around His throne in heaven. However, Satan, a beautiful angel who was decorated with all types of precious stones and was chief in the heavenlies under God, decided that he should have as much power as God. His head was lifted up in pride, and he sought to exalt himself and his kingdom above that of God (Isa. 14:12–15, Ezek. 28:11–19). As a result, a great war raged in heaven (Rev. 12:7–9), and Satan (a.k.a., the devil, Abaddon,

Apollyon, Beelzebub, Belial, Lucifer) was defeated and cast out of heaven with one-third of the angels. Jesus described this to His disciples as Satan falling like lightning from heaven (Luke 10:18).

From this beginning, the devil and the angels who followed him—known as demons or evil spirits—have sought to trick and deceive, to kill, steal, and destroy (John 10:10). Satan speaks half-truths, causes confusion, and keeps eyes from fully seeing. Genesis 3:1 states that immediately after man and woman were created and placed in the Garden of Eden, Satan appeared: "Now the serpent was more subtil than any beast of the field which the LORD God had made. And he said unto the woman, Yea, hath God said, Ye shall not eat of every tree of the garden?"

In response to these words and others that came from the trickster, the devil, the man and woman ate of the fruit that was forbidden. They then saw that they were naked and knew it. Genesis 3:22–23 records that the Lord said, "Behold, the man is become as one of us, to know good and evil: and now, lest he put forth his hand, and take also of the tree of life, and eat, and live for ever: Therefore the LORD God sent him forth from the garden of Eden, to till the ground from whence he was taken."

Thus, trickery and subtlety caused the fall of man and the expulsion of man and woman from the Garden of Eden. In addition, as soon as the fruit was eaten, the man and woman began to argue and find fault with one another. Harmony and unity had been disrupted, and now there was a division of power, a power struggle between the man and woman.

Other punishments also followed the disobedience of the man and the woman in the Garden of Eden. For the woman, the pain of childbearing would be multiplied and her desire would be for her husband, though he would rule over her. The ground was cursed, and in sorrow the man would have to work to bring forth food. And of course, the Lord sent them forth out of the beautiful garden where they had everything in place and did not have to want for anything. Because of their disobedience, they had to be removed.

The sin that occurred in the Garden of Eden is something like going into a major department store with everything—every appliance, every clothing article, everything you would want to eat—and being told to help yourself to everything but one item. Because of the inquisitiveness of our nature, we are torn up inside by the warning against taking the very thing that is forbidden. Once we touch, handle, and taste that which is forbidden, we find that it does not bring the joy, pleasure, and satisfaction we once thought it would.

Or it may be like the study hall in which students are forbidden to have gum or candy. For the disobedient student, satisfaction comes by slowly unwrapping a piece of gum or a piece of candy and enjoying and savoring the flavor as the teacher slowly looks around to see who is chewing gum or eating candy. If the student has cleverly hidden the gum or candy under his tongue and gets away with one piece, he has to try another because it is exciting just to know that he is sneaking—stealing—something he really should not have at that particular time.

This is the way evil began in the Garden of Eden. If we

have something that is forbidden, it tends to draw us to it. But when we take it, the cost is so great, so terrible, and sometimes irreversible. Surely, we must count up the cost before we take that which is forbidden. It will place us under the protection of Christ and good spiritual forces as we face evil spirits in the world around us.

Exploring the Spirit World

As we explore the spirit world in this book, we will begin in Part I by learning about angels, evil spirits, and the significant spiritual warfare in which spiritual leaders are engaged. In Part II, we will identify specific spirits that the enemy uses in his attempts to steal, kill, and destroy (John 10:10). We will first discuss many of the works of the flesh that are listed in Galatians 5:19–21, and we will also address other sources of spiritual vulnerability. Three appendices at the end of the book will supplement this material.

Part III will direct our attention to God's plan for covenant relationship with us and His provision for healing the spiritual brokenness we face in our lives and our relationships. And Part IV will describe how God blesses us with all spiritual blessings through relationship with Him. It will point us to the bottom line—that we do what God says and enter into all that He has for us by walking with Him and opening ourselves to Him in wholehearted worship.

It is my hope that you come to understand how to guard your mind and the importance of doing so, for it is the gateway to receiving evil spirits and angelic help, and physical as well as spiritual healing and deliverance.

PART I

LIFE IN THE SPIRIT WORLD

1

THE MINISTRY OF ANGELS

A 1980 GALLOP POLL suggested that 20 million people have survived a brush with death and said that 8 million of them insist that angelic beings aided them in that experience. Most people who had a near-death experience reported the same thing. They felt their body being separated from their spirit and essentially left their body and traveled in a tunnel for some time. They then experienced music, wind, and an overwhelming sense of love and peace. Most of them describe an angelic being who gave them a choice to either go forward or go back to the life they once had.[1]

Dr. Melvin Morse, a pediatrician, has collected hundreds of stories of children who have encountered angels and experienced miraculous healings. He has told of a five-year-old girl who was dead when she was brought into the hospital. After she came back to life, she said that she went to be with the angels and they told her it was not her time. They explained that her mother was going to have a little boy and she had to go back and help her mother. The doctor asked her to draw everything that had happened to her, even her spirit leaving her body, and she did it with amazing detail.[2]

In another account related to angels, a corporate executive who was a marathon runner fell dead during a marathon race and was taken to the emergency room. His spirit left his body and he went through a forest and met his guardian angel. After his angel talked to what appeared to be another group of angels, he came back to the man and told him it was not yet his time to die. Rather, he had work to do.[3]

Angels are spiritual beings created by God. Psalm 148:1–5 includes angels in a list of God's created works, and Hebrews 1:14 declares that they are "ministering spirits, sent forth to minister for them who shall be heirs of salvation." They are for us who believe, and they are there for us whenever we need them. The apostle Peter spoke about the interest angels have in God's ministry in our lives.

> Unto whom it was revealed, that not unto themselves, but unto us they did minister the things, which are now reported unto you by them that have preached the gospel unto you with the Holy Ghost sent down from heaven; which things the angels desire to look into.
>
> —1 Peter 1:12

Luke 15:10 gives us a picture of the angels' interest in us when it shows the joy they feel when one sinner repents: "There is joy in the presence of the angels of God over one sinner that repenteth." The jubilation that occurs in the heavenly realm when one person comes to Christ is almost a power surge. It shows how deeply the angels are concerned about our affairs, what we are doing, and what we are not doing.

Angels are ready to intervene and help us. Even as believers, we oftentimes feel that we are all alone and that no one is looking out for us and our concerns. However, there is hope. God has given angels much power and authority in both the heavenly and the earthly realms. They, under the directions of the Lord Jesus Christ, do intercede on our behalf. We strengthen angels to do the will of the Father and to work on our behalf by expressing faith as it is described in Mark 11:23, John 15:7, and Hebrews 11:1. By righteous living and by believing, thinking, and speaking good, positive things, we can encourage angels to move on our behalf and do the impossible for us.

Characteristics of Angels

Angels are immortal. As Jesus taught in Luke 20:36, they cannot die. They live forever, and we therefore have no reason to fear that they will be destroyed or diminished in number. They are numerous, and in fact they are innumerable. Hebrews 12:22 says, "But ye are come unto mount Sion, and unto the city of the living God, the heavenly Jerusalem, and to an innumerable company of angels." Angels are sexless, as Jesus told us in Matthew 22:30: "They neither marry, nor are given in marriage."

The Bible reveals that angels are holy. They were created to be holy, to serve the living God, the King of kings and the Lord of lords. Jesus told us this in Matthew 25:31, "When the Son of man shall come in his glory, and all the holy angels with him, then shall he sit upon the throne of his glory." Because they are holy, angels cannot tolerate anything that is not holy.

And, of course, angels are wise. As a wise woman from Tekoah told King David in 2 Samuel 14:17, "The word of my lord the king shall now be comfortable: for as an angel of God, so is my lord the king to discern good and bad: therefore the LORD thy God will be with thee." In verse 20 she added, "My lord is wise, according to the wisdom of an angel of God, to know all things that are in the earth." This does not mean that angels are perfect. Speaking of God, Job 4:18 says, "Behold, he put no trust in his servants; and his angels he charged with folly." As we have already seen, Satan is an angel who rose up against God and tried to overthrow his throne.

First Thessalonians 4:16 reveals that there is a hierarchy of angels. When Jesus comes again with "the voice of the archangel," this will show the archangel's place of command among the angelic host. Seraphims, which are described in Isaiah 6:2–3, are part of this hierarchy. Revelation 4:8 gives a similar picture of angels that are full of eyes and do not rest day or night. They praise the Lord twenty-four hours a day and are at His disposal.

Psalm 103:20 says, "Bless the LORD, ye his angels, that excel in strength, that do his commandments, hearkening unto the voice of his word." This shows that angels are extremely strong, able to do things that a mere human being is not able to do. Since they are spiritual beings, we recognize that this strength and power is divinely connected to the Lord. Angels receive their instructions and strength from the Lord, who made them.

Furthermore, angels are considered to be among the elect. The apostle Paul wrote in 1 Timothy 5:21:

> I charge thee before God, and the Lord Jesus Christ, and the elect angels, that thou observe these things without preferring one before another, doing nothing by partiality.

There are chosen, elect angels that are charged with specific duties. An example of this occurred in Daniel 10:10–14, when Daniel prayed and his answer was held up twenty-one days by the prince of the kingdom of Persia. The Lord chose Michael, one of the chief princes, to help Daniel by overcoming the spiritual opposition against him. God chooses and sends whomever He will from the hierarchy in his angelic realm to take authority over any obstacle that blocks what He wants. Whatever may block His intentions or stop the progression of His Word, He provides an elect angel that can effectively and efficiently do the required job.

Psalm 103:20 teaches that angels are obedient to God and His Word, and their ministry reflects the fact that they are meek. We see this in Jude 1:9:

> Yet Michael the archangel, when contending with the devil he disputed about the body of Moses, durst not bring against him a railing accusation, but said, The Lord rebuke thee.

When Michael, the archangel, judicially argued with the devil over the body of Moses, he respected the leadership and authority the devil once had with God. He dared not—he would not—use carnal warfare and bring condemnation or even accusation against the devil for the wrong he had done by rising up against God. Instead, in the spirit of meekness, he used spiritual warfare and simply used the authoritative and all-powerful name of Jesus to win not only the battle but the war against the devil. He realized that he had no choice but to use the strength and wisdom and knowledge of the One who gave him the power to do what he was doing.

Angels bring people together for the purposes the Lord deems necessary. When God wanted Philip to witness to the Ethiopian treasurer, "The angel of the Lord spake unto Philip, saying, Arise, and go toward the south unto the way that goeth down from Jerusalem unto Gaza, which is desert" (Acts 8:26). Another ministry of angels is to direct our paths and tell us where to go and how to go safely. Many people have told stories of how a voice—whether it be the Holy Spirit, an angel, or someone who has called them—told them, "Don't go that way." Many accidents have been avoided, many lives have been saved because of direction from angels.

How Angels Minister to Believers

The Bible tells numerous stories that illustrate important roles angels have in the lives of believers: to provide, deliver, encourage, guide, and comfort. In 1 Kings 19:1–8 Elijah ran from Jezebel because she threatened to take his life and went into the wilderness. There, he sat under a juniper tree and asked the Lord to take his life. Tired and hungry, he slept under the tree until an angel touched him and told him to get up and eat and drink the food and water he had for him. He went to sleep again, and the angel came again with food and water. Elijah was able to go forty days and forty nights on the food the angel provided for him that day.

Psalm 34:7 promises, "The angel of the LORD encampeth round about them that fear him, and delivereth them." I experienced this very personally when I was heading to church one beautiful Sunday morning. The heel of my shoe got caught in a crack on the stairs of an apartment complex, and I began to fall face-forward. At the very moment I began to holler for help, someone turned me around, held me in mid air, and gently laid me on my back on the ground.

My husband and my daughter were quite a distance in front of me. After my husband ran up to me, he asked, "Did you see that?"

"Yes," I replied, "that was my angel." No one was close by to catch me, but an invisible force caught me that day and has been catching me every day.

Daniel 6:22 shows angels are with us to protect us from harm or hurt that the enemy or circumstances may bring. Daniel was faithful to pray to God, the great I AM, three times a day even though the king had made a decree that forbade anyone to pray to anyone except him for thirty days. As punishment for this, he was then thrown into the lions' den. However, God sent an angel who closed the mouths of the lions, and no hurt came to Daniel.

In Acts 12, King Herod put Peter in prison and assigned sixteen soldiers to guard him. The night before he was to be brought to trial, as intercessory prayer was continually made for him, the angel of the Lord came to him. The chains that bound Peter fell away, and the angel led him out of the prison and into the city. After walking with Peter only briefly on the street, the angel left him, and Peter realized that an angel had delivered him from the hand of Herod.

Centuries later, in the early 1900s, Bishop Charles Harrison Mason, the founder of the Church of God in Christ, was jailed in Lexington, Mississippi, for preaching the gospel. In response to this, the saints continually prayed, and Bishop Mason prayed. And when a wind came and took the top off the jailhouse where Bishop Mason was, the authorities were glad to release him. Many believed that angels came to his rescue as a sign of who he was in Christ.[4] Matthew 24:31 says, "And he shall send his angels with a great sound of a trumpet, and they shall gather together his elect from the four winds, from one end of heaven to the other."

Genesis 21:14–19 tells how the angel of God gave encouragement and guidance to Hagar and Ishmael when Abraham had sent them away into the wilderness and their water was spent. Verse 17 says that "God heard the voice of the lad" and called to Hagar out of heaven, asking, "What aileth thee, Hagar? fear not; for God hath heard the voice of the lad where he is." He encouraged her with the promise to make Ishmael a great nation and opened her eyes to see a well of water.

We see another example of the ministry of guidance through angels in Genesis 24. When Abraham sent his servant to his father's homeland to bring back a wife for Isaac, he said in verse 40, "The LORD, before whom I walk, will send his angel with thee, and prosper thy way; and thou shalt take a wife for my son of my kindred, and of my father's house." An angel guided the servant to find a wife for Isaac.

The story of the shipwreck Paul and his shipmates survived in Acts 27 shows how angels provide comfort in the time of distress, pain, and sorrow. Because the centurion had listened to the master and the owner of the ship instead of Paul, the ship in which they were sailing was caught in a storm that threatened to destroy the ship and all those who were in it. On one of the long, anxious days when the storm was at its worst, Paul stood up in the midst of the ship and told everyone that "the angel of God, whose I am, and whom I serve" (v. 23) had come to him and said that there would be no loss of life. Because of the hope the angel provided, Paul offered words of good cheer that came true.

Angels May Take a Human Form

Angels can be invisible to people when they intervene in various situations here on Earth. Numbers 22:22–31 describes how the angel of the Lord was invisible to Balaam when he smote his donkey three times because it refused to proceed on the road ahead. Balaam's eyes were blinded to what the donkey could see—the angel of Lord, who stood in his way with a drawn sword in hand. Finally, the third time Balaam beat his donkey, the Lord opened the animal's mouth to speak to his master. The Lord also opened Balaam's eyes to see the angel of the Lord, who told him that he opposed Balaam's journey "because thy way is perverse before me" (v. 23).

Angels are also able to incarnate, to take a human form, as we learn in Genesis 18 and 19. Three "men" came to tell Abraham of the impending birth of his son Isaac in Genesis 18:1–15. Abraham and Sarah were old and well stricken in age by this time, and Sarah laughed within herself at the thought of having a child. In response to this, the Lord Himself, one of the three men, asked, "Is any thing too hard for the LORD? At the time appointed I will return unto thee, according to the time of life, and Sarah shall have a son" (Gen. 18:14).

The men then turned toward Sodom, which the Lord planned to destroy because of the wickedness of the people. However, because of the faithfulness of Abraham, He sent the two angels to rescue Abraham's loved ones before this destruction occurred. Sodom and Gomorrah were particularly wicked cities, and the thing that was emphasized in this scripture was the sin of homosexuality. The men of Sodom saw the angels go to Lot's house and followed them, seeking their presence so that they might entertain them.

Even though Lot stepped outside his house to offer the men of Sodom his virgin daughters, they refused them and tried to force their way into Lot's house. The angels quickly drew Lot into the house and smote the men at the door with blindness so that they were unable to find it. Then the angels told Lot to gather all his family and get out of the city because they had to destroy it for its wickedness. Early the next morning, they told Lot to leave with haste and not to tarry, lest he be consumed with the other people in the city. Even with that warning, Lot still lingered, and the angels took the hands of Lot and his wife and his two daughters, and brought them out of the city.

One of the angels warned Lot and his family not to look back but to head straight for the mountains. Then the Lord rained brimstone and fire upon Sodom and Gomorrah, and all those who were in the city were destroyed. Lot's wife looked back at this, and she became a pillar of salt. Even though God had warned of the coming judgment and extended mercy for her escape, she felt that she had to look back, and she herself was destroyed. This is a lesson for all of us. Yes, it is important to understand and appreciate the deliverance God has accomplished in our lives. However, we should never look back to dwell or even want to linger in the past from which He has rescued us.

Genesis 18 and 19 show the importance of angels in taking on human form to be messengers and give us leadership and guidance. The Lord sends angels of strength and chooses them for specific missions, to carry out his bidding when His children are in trouble and need to be delivered from destruction. He provides angels to be intercessors and speak His message to us with the proper authority to deal with the specific obstacles that are interfering with His work.

Angels Execute God's Judgment

Angels are at work not only in the lives of believers, but also in the execution of God's judgment for sin. As we learn in Genesis 19:13, angels were ministers of God's destruction of Sodom and Gomorrah. In the song of Deborah and Barak, the angel of the Lord cursed Meroz "because they came not to the help of the LORD, to the help of the LORD against the mighty" (Judg. 5:23). We can cause the angels to curse us if we do not help when the Lord instructs us to help His people.

Second Samuel 24 tells how the anger of the Lord was kindled against David because he sinned by numbering the people of Israel. As a result, the Lord, by the hand of an angel, sent a pestilence upon Israel. Yet, God's mercy endured, and the angel of the Lord was stayed by the voice of the Lord. Second Samuel 24:16 says:

> And when the angel stretched out his hand upon Jerusalem to destroy it, the LORD repented him of the evil, and said to the angel that destroyed the people, It is enough: stay now thine hand. And the angel of the LORD was by the threshingplace of Araunah the Jebusite.

Sudden acts of execution have been credited to angels. Acts 12:23 records that "the angel of the Lord smote [Herod], because he gave not God the glory: and he was eaten of worms, and gave up the ghost." Herod died because he allowed the people to portray him as a god and took the glory that belonged to the Lord. We, too, must be careful that we do not take the glory, honor, and praises that belong to the Lord. We must always be careful to point others to the Lord, God Almighty, rather than point to ourselves or take credit for the miracles and His good and perfect gifts. Psalm 115:1 says, "Not unto us, O LORD, not unto us, but unto thy name give glory, for thy mercy, and for thy truth's sake."

In Psalm 35:5–6, David described the angel of the Lord as one who persecutes those who were persecuting him: "Let them be as chaff before the wind: and let the angel of the LORD chase them. Let their way be dark and slippery: and let the angel of the LORD persecute them." This teaches us that angels have a role in the persecution of those who are in darkness, those who are unbelievers, those who are on the devil's payroll.

While we must recognize the role of angels in judgment for sin, we do not have to live in fear about this. We can open our hearts in faith to Christ and receive the ministry they give to believers. What we say, what we do, what we think in our hearts, and the praises we send up to the Lord God Almighty will give strength to the angels.

Angels were created both to praise the Lord and also to be of service to all mankind. We should appreciate the fact that the Lord cared enough about us to allow angels to be here on Earth with us to help us and aid us on our way. As an expression of this appreciation, we must be careful how we entertain a stranger, because we may be entertaining an angel unaware (Heb. 13:2). The person who has a friendly smile; the person who gives you wise guidance; the person who looks like someone you knew before; the person who makes you feel warm inside, comfortable, and at peace—this person may be an angel.

A Testimony of an Angel's Ministry

In "My Conversation with the Trumpet Man," a woman told how God sends us angels even when we really do not want to hear them.[5] She was devastated because her children were both suffering serious illness, and fear had essentially overwhelmed her. Two of her three children had been diagnosed with Epstein-Barr virus, an infection that causes mononucleosis and is similar to chronic fatigue syndrome. The joints swell up and one is completely exhausted and requires a lot of bed rest. The thing that really hurt her was that her oldest daughter came down with a parasitic disease in her gastrointestinal tract and had to have a long-term course of antibiotics that she was told could cause hearing loss.

Because of her great concern about these things, the woman was not sleeping or eating, and she had lost forty pounds in about twelve weeks. Her hair was coming out, and her doctor advised her that she was going to have a nervous breakdown if she did not calm down and stop worrying about the difficulties in her life and her family. This lady was exhausted, and she felt she would lose her mind. Then she met and had nine conversations with an African-American man who was playing a trumpet by the seashore of Staten Island, New York.

The man, whose hair was fleeced with gray, played his horn magnificently. However, she felt that he was just another homeless person playing for spare change as she noticed that he wore a raggedy, oversized coat. When he stopped playing for a minute, she told him, "You are not going to make any money down here."

He looked at her and replied, "I play for God's ears, not tourists, not gamblers, just for God."

When she told him he was essentially wasting his time, the

man responded, "Lady, you are whining. God does not like whining."

She questioned whether God had personally told him this, and he said, yes He had. He continued to tell her that he and God had a good personal relationship, and they were good friends. "We talk all the time," he added and then explained how God talked to him everyday. He expressed thanks to God for taking care of him and for all the wonderful gifts He had given him.

The woman immediately challenged him because she wondered how he could be thankful when he had nothing to be thankful for. He replied, "Well, I have my health; I have two shoes, even though they are mismatched; I have an oversized coat, but there are a lot of people who are not even warm."

Finally, with a heart that felt God would never hear her prayer, the woman essentially said, "Why am I wasting my time talking to this man who is being thankful for a whole lot of nothing? He has nothing."

As she began to walk away, he bellowed out, "Lady, your children are going to be fine. They are going to be absolutely fine."

"I never told him about my children," she thought, and immediately looked back toward the man. However, he was no longer there. She asked people on the beach if they had seen him, and no one had ever seen him before. She wondered if she was losing her mind.

However, as she searched the beach, the woman found the footprints of the man with mismatched shoes. And as the trumpet man said, her two children were fine. The daughter she had feared would lose her hearing did not. God had sent an angel even to speak healing for her children and hope for her heart. She had learned the angels are there for us.

Frederick Douglass said, "Without a struggle, there can be no progress."[6] In Genesis 32:24–32, Jacob wrestled with the angel until daybreak. As he wrestled with the angel, he was also wrestling with himself, his inner fears, and his insecurities. He was wrestling with the wrongs he had done by being a trickster, stealing his brother's birthright, and taking the blessing his father intended to give to his brother. After he wrestled, Jacob not only won the battle, but he was determined that he would not let the angel go until he blessed him.

Jacob's name was changed. He gained the truth and became a new man, a new creation who was willing to face his failures, the wrongs he had done, and also his brother. God turned a situation in which he thought his brother would be an enemy into a meeting with a loving brother who just wanted to make things right between them. Sometimes we have to wrestle with an angel or wrestle with ourselves to get things right.

Personal Experiences with Angels

As I close this chapter, I want to share three precious personal experiences I have had with angels. First, after I completed my medical school training, I went to the first day of my surgical rotation in residency. I was very excited about an open heart surgery in which I was going to assist, but I could not find my scrubs. I prayed about this because, if I couldn't find them, I would have to return home, disappointed, and even tell my peers that I did not attend the surgery. I was so heartbroken because there was no one anywhere who could give me any scrubs.

As I walked down the hospital hallway, its corridors waxed to a T, I cried out to God, "Lord, please help me. I really want to be in on the surgery."

A lady appeared out of nowhere smiling wonderfully and sweetly, and asked me, "Do you need some scrubs?"

"Yes," I replied. "I do."

"What size do you need?"

I told her, and she gave me a set of scrubs. The unusual thing about her appearance was not that she was there, but rather that others weren't. The regional cardiac center was normally a busy place, but apart from her and me, it was isolated. As she spoke, I felt warmth, love, and peace coming from her. I knew I had seen her before, but it was almost as if I was blinded to who she was. After I gladly put the scrubs on, I turned back to say thank you, and she smiled. When I turned toward her again, however, she was nowhere to be seen. The surgery was a wonderful thing, the most beautiful experience I have ever seen and assisted in. But when I came back after the surgery, no one had ever seen this lady. I was never able to find her. She was one of my angels.

Another experience happened the last time I saw a man who once came by the church campus and outreach office quite regularly for an encouraging word. Although it was obvious that he lacked some of his mental facilities, he always smelled good and had a clear countenance and a very humble spirit.

On that last time I saw him he asked me for some money to get something to eat. In response to the Lord's urging, I gave him all that was in my hand. "Thank you," he said. Then he looked at me with all the love that he could muster, and asked, "Who loves me?"

"Jesus loves you," I replied, "and I love you too."

"That's right," he agreed. Then he continued, "Where am I going one day?"

"You are going to heaven one day," I answered.

He smiled and walked away, his countenance glowing. He was an angel unaware, needing help so that he would be able to tell the Father that someone who helped him needed a blessing. That day I learned that our giving should lift up the name of the Lord and be a representation of His majesty, His beauty, and all His splendor.

The Lord always sends a messenger to us on our journey of life. It may have the form of a human, of flowers, or a voice. Or it may be a beautiful peacock that spreads his tail feathers, with color so dashing, so beautiful that we must stand in awe.

I remember when a little bird with beautiful, multiple colors stood on the stoop by my office window, as if to say, "I came to say good morning." The bird appeared healthy, strong, and had no noticeable deficit. Many people came by just to look at the bird. Everyone who saw it immediately began to smile, and most stayed for several minutes before moving on. It stood there, and no matter who came or went, it stood there. Even when we put food out for it, the bird stayed there and refused to leave. But when we went out one morning, it had flown away. It had delivered a message, "I am here to brighten up your day," and now the time had come for it to go.

2

THE WORK OF EVIL SPIRITS

When Satan fell from heaven, he took one-third of the angels with him to serve him rather than the Lord (Ezek. 28:11–19). These fallen angels—evil spirits or demons—are numerous. As fallen angels, they, like the angels who serve God, are powerful. They also operate in a hierarchy, an authoritative order in the army of the devil.

What can spirits do? What are their abilities? They can drive, torment, and possess human beings. They can also recognize Christ and His presence in another person. When Jesus was teaching in the synagogue at Capernaum in Mark 1:21–26, a man who had an unclean spirit cried out and said, "Let us alone; what have we to do with thee, thou Jesus of Nazareth? Have you come to destroy us?" Jesus rebuked the unclean spirit and told him to hold his peace and come out of the man. Of course, he had no choice but to do as Christ said.

We know that the devil recognizes one who does not have strength in Christ Jesus. He knows if someone does not have the

Holy Spirit. When Paul was performing miracles at Ephesus, some of the "vagabond Jewish exorcists" felt they could imitate Paul and cast out a demon just as he had. Acts 19:14–15 says, "And there were seven sons of one Sceva, a Jew, and chief of the priests, which did so. And the evil spirit answered and said, Jesus I know, and Paul I know; but who are ye?" The man in whom the evil spirit lived leaped upon them and overcame them, essentially beating them up until they ran out of the house wounded and naked.

Demons can fight, provoke, and push. They can cause anger to the point that it leads to violence that can actually hurt or destroy someone. If a person has an unclean spirit, the act of violence and the strength to do it are much, much greater than one's natural human ability. We know that demons are powerful because nobody could bind or tie down the man who was tormented with an unclean spirit and came out of the tombs when Jesus and His disciples came to the country of the Gadarenes in Mark 5:1–14.

When the man saw Jesus, he ran to Him and had no choice but to worship Him. He said, "What have I to do with thee, Jesus, thou Son of the most high God? I adjure thee by God, that thou torment me not" (Mark 5:7). Jesus simply said, "Come out of the man, thou unclean spirit" (v. 8). He further demanded that the unclean spirit give his name, and he replied, "Legion: for we are many" (v. 9). The demons were not only subject to Christ, but they were forced to speak and answer His questions because of the power and authority He carried.

The demons begged and pleaded that Jesus would not send them out of that area. They requested instead to go into a nearby herd of swine that were feeding on the mountain, and Jesus granted this. The man was freed as the herd ran violently down a steep place into the sea, and about two thousand swine died.

God has given us the same authority Jesus had in this story. While demons do have authority and power to drive, torment, and possess people, we who belong to Christ have His authority and power over demons. This power was given in Matthew 10:1, "And when [Jesus] had called unto him his twelve disciples, he gave them power against unclean spirits, to cast them out, and to heal all manner of sickness and all manner of disease."

Demons are clearly under the influence and direction of Satan himself. In Matthew 12:24, the Pharisees accused Jesus of casting out devils "by Beelzebub the prince of the devils." They said that He was a part of Satan's camp. However, Jesus clearly showed that He cast out devils by the Spirit of God. He explained to the Pharisees that Satan cannot cast out Satan. If a person is of Satan, he will join Satan's force. He cannot cast out a demon or a devil. The demon in him will recognize the demon in the other person, and they will join together to be stronger. One who is possessed by a demon cannot cast out that same demon in another person.

Because of this, one who is seeking prayer for deliverance should not ask someone who is possessed with the same demon. One young lady who was divorced sought prayer for her struggles with thoughts of fornication. She did not know that the man who prayed for her had a problem with a lustful spirit and had also given himself to multiple affairs. After prayer, her struggle became so great and almost overwhelmed her to the point that she wanted to have an affair. After much prayer and counseling, she understood that the lustful spirit had been transferred to her. The very thing she was seeking deliverance from was strengthened by the prayer of someone who possessed that spirit.

Another person was not so fortunate. A young lady who was married to a very faithful minister received prayer from someone who had problems with multiple affairs. Although she did not understand why she was doing it, she began to have an affair with another man. Even though she had never done anything like it before, the transference of spirits led to a tragic end for her marriage.

The Transference of Spirits

The transference of spirits is a reality that poses great danger to us. In one example of this, a young lady who had been abused as a child would attempt to beat someone up every time she became angry. One time, she violently beat her child. She was so ashamed and hurt that she did not know what to do, and she sought help. Although she stopped beating her child, she then began to attack her husband and beat him to the point that he sought a divorce. Even though she was not a large lady, the strength and the intensity of the beatings were so great that her husband could not take it. She was not able to control her anger until she was totally delivered from demonic control.

John Hagee, the pastor of Cornerstone Church in San Antonio, Texas, has recounted another story that shows how dangerous the transference of spirits is. He has quite often told how one of his members went to see the movie *The Exorcist* and after viewing it, began to take on the characteristics of the person who was possessed. This shows that we have to be careful what our children watch on television, in movies, and at theatrical plays. We must be selective in their grooming and create an environment that will nurture them to be Christlike as they grow and mature.

In yet another instance of transference, some children were playing at a church service in which some nasty evil spirits were cast out of a woman. The parents did not cover the children during the deliverance prayer, and their daughter started acting out and doing bizarre things after the family returned home. The evil spirits had transferred into her, and she began to do things she had never done before and say things that were very inappropriate. The parents were advised to pray for their daughter and to acknowledge the presence of the Lord in her and through her. As they did, deliverance came to her and it has never recurred.

This is one of many instances that shows the importance of laying hands on children and praying a covering over them when they are in the same room where prayer is being offered for people possessed with demonic spirits. Children are very open and very susceptible to unclean spirits. We must protect them and *every* believer with a prayer covering to guard against every evil attack of the enemy. Spirits are not just superstition or spooky stuff out of a fairy tale. They are very real. We have victory over the evil one through the spirit of Christ within us.

The Vulnerability of an Open Spirit

We can leave our spirits open to attack through sinful acts, including feelings of unforgiveness. As the Holy Spirit says stop, we must learn to yield to Him. Jesus warned about this in Matthew 12:43–45, where he described how a man who was delivered from an unclean spirit but was still an empty house for that spirit and seven more wicked spirits to return and inhabit him. When we are cleansed from sin, the spirits that are cast out will search for a place to go. If they cannot enter any other house, they will return to the place where they had originally been. They can only enter the original house or person if there is an opening.

One tragic example of the vulnerability of an open spirit is the story of what happened when teenage girl acquired a demon and came to the altar for prayer one Sunday morning. "I want to burn," she began to say. "I want to go to hell. Leave me alone." The senior pastor, who at that time was young in spiritual matters, asked the pastor who had experience dealing with demons to stop praying for the young lady, and he did.

That same night, however, the demon transferred to her brother, who became angry with his father simply because he asked him to stop talking on the phone. With no prior history of violence, the young man killed his father and walked away as if he had done nothing. The sister was free because she had been used as a transport, while her brother had been open to the spirit of murder and had yielded to it because of anger.

In response to this, the senior pastor immediately and publicly apologized to the pastor who had been praying with the young woman. "I should have allowed you to cast that demon out," he said. He knew that if the demon had been cast out, the young girl would not have taken it home to her brother.

Another instance of demonic activity related to an open spirit occurred when a man and three women, all believers, were greeting one another before a meeting to discuss a business venture. As they did, a shadow of a man slightly shorter than the man entered him, and he immediately became very angry and belligerent for no reason. He verbally attacked two of the women until the shadow left him. The two women stood in amazement at what had happened to the sweet and gentle person who had suddenly become a roaring lion. The man had an open spirit due to having multiple affairs with various women, and he had no knowledge of what had occurred.

God is able to intervene and bring victory in situations where there is spiritual weakness because of an open spirit. In a church meeting someone began to rebuke the spirit of death, and the congregation joined in to ask the Lord not to allow this spirit to overtake any of the believers who had traveled to the conference. During this time, a woman who was there experienced a generalized weakness all over her body. As she explained it, she could feel her body leaving this world but could not cry out for assistance and felt helpless.

While this was happening, the Lord touched another woman who had been at the front of the room with her back turned to the woman who was dying. The second woman walked back to the first woman, who was actually dying but then gained strength and told what had occurred in her body.

In another story that reveals God's ministry of life, a very pretty, well-educated woman was rescued from death after her multiple affairs and several failed marriages brought her to the point of hopelessness. She was very lonely, and as she lay in her bed feeling very sorry for herself, depression set in. With all her heart, she desired to die and leave this world and all the pain of life. Though she was sure she was not asleep, her spirit began to slowly leave her physical body.

She drifted like this for several minutes until she had to make a conscious decision for life or death. She had opened herself to sadness, depression, and then death. Then she saw a woman praying for her and asking her not to leave yet. At that exact time, the woman she saw was indeed interceding for her in prayer. She said no to death, and her spirit returned to her as she repented for not being thankful for what she had. The Lord blessed her the next year with a marriage to a husband who was a wonderful, very successful believer and cherished their relationship.

One Christian leader was deeply involved in building the kingdom for the Lord, and souls were being saved hundreds at a time through his ministry. However, his spirit was open to the point that he had multiple affairs. A woman who he normally would not have looked at came into his life at a weak moment and changed his world for a lifetime. He left the church he had built from the ground—and his wife—to be with the other woman.

After staying with this woman for about a year, he wondered why he had left his wife. He tried to go back to her, but it was not as easy as he thought. It took about five years before she would receive him back, and his children were without their father for seven years. The cost of his mistakes was devastating to the flock, and his church was completely destroyed as its members went to other ministries. His actions caused many to distrust in Christian leadership.

Pastors and other leaders especially have to be extremely careful after they minister because their spirit is very open. One should not do a lot of mingling after he delivers the Word, but should be allowed to rest and replenish for a while. One pastor who had multiple affairs recounts that after speaking on Sunday many women would approach him for sexual favors. He said he could not refuse them and that it was like he had no will to say no. He was ashamed to tell anyone or share what was happening to him until the women started to brag about their times with him. He admitted that he was wrong and lost his pride when he had to confess all. With God's help, he recovered his family after seeking the Lord with repentance.

In a final story that shows the vulnerability of an open spirit, a well-known pastor who had a very successful, thriving ministry for over twenty years prayed for his congregation's deliverance from many bondages and homosexuality. He was married and never had any desires for anyone except his wife. Although he had no desire toward a man, he felt a spirit of homosexuality come upon him because he had become over-tired and had not stopped to refuel spiritually.

He found himself restless and anxious not knowing what to do about his most awkward situation. As he reached out for clergy all over the body of Christ to pray for him, his deliverance came. He did not consider pride or any consequences that would happen because some who were weak would talk about him. Instead, he boldly asked the body of Christ to pray. He opened his spirit to receive God's ministry through the church.

Evil Spirits May Attack in Force

Although I have never seen it documented, I find it amazing that various evil spirits manifest themselves all over the world at exactly the same time. It is almost as if they are released periodically. If one person is diagnosed with cancer, there are usually multiples of it all over. If there is a rash of murders in one area, it is as if a murdering spirit has gone out and also spread its evil wherever there is an open door. I have noticed that when there are a number of murders on TV, the spirit of murder will be imitated in various areas of the country. After the Columbine murders, similar incidents followed.

Is this a coincidence, or is it the fact that spirits are unified and therefore go out in force? There are spirits who agree to do damage to people and therefore are released by their leader to raise havoc on particular people at particular times. The Bible records how this happened near the end of King Ahab's reign over Israel:

> And the Lord said, Who shall persuade Ahab, that he may go up and fall at Ramothgilead? And one said on this manner, and another said on that manner. And there came forth a spirit, and stood before the Lord, and said, I will persuade him. And the Lord said unto him, Wherewith? And he

> said, I will go forth, and I will be a lying spirit in the mouth of all his prophets. And he said, Thou shalt persuade him, and prevail also: go forth, and do so.
>
> —1 Kings 22:20–22

When evil is present and a person has an open spirit, evil spirits can possess that person. They volunteer to inhabit various individuals when there is an opening, and they go forth as one person to possess them to an evil end.

God's Victory over Evil Spirits

God has given the believer authority over evil spirits, and I would like to share some personal experiences with this. One time I visited a woman who was hallucinating, seeing dead relatives, and experiencing minor psychoses after she had minor surgery. As I entered the room, she became perfectly clear in her thinking and told me all that had happened in her mind. I prayed with her and left her to the care of her daughter and sister.

Shortly after I left, she returned to a psychotic state. She began to hear voices and did not recognize most of the people who attempted to call or visit. Her daughter remarked that her mind was clear only while I was in the room, and I explained that every spirit is subject to the Spirit of Christ through the Holy Spirit. Therefore order must come to every place that is visited by one who possesses the power of the Spirit of the Lord.

In another instance, a man had come under the power of

witchcraft through contact with his girlfriend, who did not like the fact that he had a wife. His doctors said he was in a mental state that they could not explain by any test they had done, and his mother asked me, as a physician and a believer, to visit him. As I entered the room, he sat up and became clear and answered every question I asked. I told his mother that the Lord said he would go home in three days with a clear mind. The doctor laughed because he felt that the man would be institutionalized. In three days, however, the man went home with a clear mind free from the witchcraft spirit.

I have prayed for many homes and offices, but two of them come to mind as places that had a large number of evil spirits. As I entered one home, an invisible force stood at the entrance. I had to stop momentarily, even though there was no obvious blockade. Then, however, it was like a door opened and the forces parted so that I was allowed to enter the house. After I prayed, the forces were completely gone.

As I prayed for another house, I went into an area with movement that could not be explained by natural forces. Although nothing was seen or heard, it was like a community of people was in the room. The owner explained that the room was once a secret place where the previous resident used drugs. No one had known where the room was because it was cleverly hidden behind a sliding wall.

3

WARFARE IN HIGH PLACES

JUST AS SOCIETY and the military follow an order of command, the spirit world of good and evil also follow a line of authority. Both inside and outside the body of Christ, an organization can go no further or be elevated any higher than the spiritual authority of the person who is over that group. Not one person in the ministry can exceed the growth and development of the leadership in spiritual authority over him or her.

If a leader has any addictive problems—let's say it is overeating—and lacks discipline in this area, his flock will have problems akin to this if they remain with their shepherd. If he has a problem with lust, the flock, especially the males but also the females, will have similar problems. This is especially true if the leader continuously lays hands on his flock and gives those spirits freedom to transfer to those who are open to them.

Those who earnestly desire to go to a higher spiritual level than that of the leadership over them will usually seek another ministry, while others are content to stay where they are because they have similar addictions. Many just backslide and go back to a spiritual state that is worse than they originally were in before they received Christ; they had neither depth in the Word nor strength in the Lord. In one ministry where the leader openly engaged in promiscuous acts with various women, many of the sons lost hope.

A tragic example of this loss of hope happened in the life of a man who was completely delivered from thirty years of drug addiction through the blood of Jesus. He loved and adored his pastor to the point of saying, "I'll take a bullet for him." One day the pastor called a meeting with the man's wife and tried to seduce her in his office. Although she ran and never told her husband, he knew.

While the man was shaving one morning, he asked his wife, "Has our pastor tried to seduce you?" She began to sob and answered yes. He began drinking that day, and it lead him back to the drug addiction that had bound him before. Though he tried with all his might to come back to God, he continued to drink. He understood that it was an evil spirit in the leader, but he could not tolerate the betrayal.

If a corporation is not producing, the head of the company looks at the leaders of each group within the company and the board of directors looks at the president. If a ball team is not producing, the coach is replaced. In the body of Christ, however, most try to follow the example of David in his response to King Saul. David determined to touch not God's anointed, nor do his prophet any harm (1 Sam. 24:5–7). Many have the thought that God established Saul as king and it was up to Him to remove him in the process of time. Saul was indeed removed because David loved him, prayed for him, and ran from him. But he never lost his reverence for his leadership.

Eli was an old man when he was removed from his position and replaced by Samuel because he allowed his sons to commit sin against the Lord in the temple. He rebuked them and had the power to stop them, but he did not force the issue with them. Aaron, the brother of Moses, messed up several times, but the Lord waited until Aaron had removed his priestly garments before he died (1 Sam. 2–3; Num. 20:22–28).

The Nature of Spiritual Attacks

Ephesians 6:12 states, "For we wrestle not against flesh and blood, but against principalities, against powers, against the rulers of the darkness of this world, against spiritual wickedness in high places." I believe this shows that the devil has assigned demons in his army against each of us in our respective places in God's kingdom. Some are just coming to Christ to yield their lives to Him, while others are already in positions of leadership in Christian ministry. Yet others are about to be advanced. In each of our lives, an evil spirit comes against the purpose and destiny God has ordained for us.

Notice that the enemy's target is not a person, but God's purpose and destiny. If one has just received salvation, it may only require a private in Satan's army to cause that person to fall from grace. If someone who has only had salvation for a week speaks a simple insult to a newcomer at church, the devil plays on the fact that a "church person has done this." This may cause hurt and injury to the point that the person will not even return to church.

Some hear about the different problems within a ministry. They hear statements such as, "People have their own little group and they are not friendly," and begin to think, "Well, maybe this is not the place for me." Some go from church to church, not because of what they experience but because of comments they hear from others. These persons have no depth in their relationship with Christ, and little or no effort by the devil easily causes them to move.

A sergeant in Satan's army may be used against someone who has some small roots but lacks great depth of strength or knowledge. This person would really be hurt if he wanted to head a project but was not allowed to because he lacked the wisdom and understanding to deal with various groups of people. Or, a person who has been in ministry about a year may receive correction from the pastor and instantly take offense because of it. Such a person lacks teaching and also understanding.

Children may be affected by spirits, but they easily let most things go. When they feel rejected by their playmates, they may say, "He will not play with me," or, "He says he is not my friend." Although they feel despair and disappointment, they for the most part immediately forgive the other child when they want to play again. They tend not to hold grudges or things that happened the day before—and sometimes the minute before! All one child has to do is say, "Come on, let's play," and in most cases the other child says, "OK."

Most young children have very forgiving hearts, and we as adults should pattern ourselves after them. The spirits that attack most children are only privates in Satan's army. Some encounter abuse, neglect, and the like because, I believe, they have great purpose. The enemy attacks them early in life to prevent them from causing damage to the kingdom of evil.

As one grows under the Lord's anointing and declares the authority of the Lord, the enemy assigns a specific spirit to discourage or even stop that person's progression in the kingdom of God. This is an effort to keep the believer from walking into the airspace or dwelling place that demons inhabit. The presence of the believer causes unclean spirits to become uneasy and to tremble and leave even before a word is spoken.

The greater the Lord's anointing upon a believer, the greater will be the attack of the devil. A leader will have little trouble with the devil if he has perhaps fifty members, is satisfied with no outreach, and is more concerned about what a person wears than their soul. It is important that we show love to others, no matter what they are wearing or what they are currently doing. If one attempts to come to worship, evidently that person wants some type of change. We must not neglect to help such a person come into relationship with the Lord.

A leader who is greatly anointed by God and is very aggressive in loving the Lord and loving His sheep will come against many spirits. The spirits of lust, power, or greed generally oppose such a leader, although all of them are not necessary at this level of the authoritative ladder. All of us are tempted, and even Jesus was tempted by Satan after He fasted for forty days

(Matt. 4:1–11). Temptation will come, but we must resist it to accomplish the purpose the Lord has ordained for our lives.

God has set a destiny for each of us, and we are the only ones who can change what has been put in place if we disobey the Word and will of the Lord. This is what happened to the children of Israel, whom God promised to take to a land flowing with milk and honey. After their repeated disobedience, the Lord denied a generation from going into that land, but promised that their children would be allowed to enter it. In Numbers 14, the Lord said, "I have to break this promise because you did not keep your end of the covenant."

An evil spirit attempts to take over the whole mind-set of an individual. It does this as aggressively as possible with a temptation that comes at a time of weakness. It is like a seed that is planted and then yields much fruit. The entrance of one evil spirit opens the door to other spirits that are much worse than the initial one. The purpose of that spirit is to eventually control and drive the individual until he is enslaved and serves every desire of the evil spirit.

When this happens, one no longer has a purpose except to satisfy the longing and craving created by the evil spirit in control. The Lord is no longer the priority, for the hunger must be satisfied. The further one gives himself to satisfying his hunger for evil, the greater distance he seeks to put between himself and the Lord. However, as one steps closer to the Lord, the less he needs the evil things that have been occupying the time and space in his life.

Spiritual Attacks Against Leadership

The devil seeks to bring an unclean spirit against the head of every organization. If the head is dysfunctional, the whole body is off track because it functions and carries out its duties in response to the head. If the brain is off, the body is following the faulty commands of the head. This is why it is so important to pray for all leadership in the country and in all organizations. We can actually cause heaven to intervene in many situations if we offer prayer rather than criticism in response to decisions and problems that leaders face.

Prayer for deliverance, not to mention divine guidance, is always in order. Not only will our leaders be blessed but also when we come into a leadership position, others will pray for us. Specific spirits are set to attack newcomers and lay members, while stronger spirits attempt to devour deacons and evangelists. Even stronger ones are at work against pastors and district leaders. The strongest of spirits seek to hinder and destroy any leader who is over a national or international work.

The enemy's effort is not to kill and destroy the head but the whole body. Logic tells us to aim for the middle of the head, as David did with Goliath, not to just wound the body but to completely knock it out. Wherever we have a slight weakness, we must cover it with the blood at all times. If the Lord has delivered one from lust, he must guard against being too friendly with the opposite sex. If one has a problem with power, much fasting and prayer must be done to keep the flesh subjected to the Lord's control.

The higher one is elevated before the eyes of man in the natural realm, the greater the attack of the spirits. Many look at people in leadership with critical eyes and say that they would do things differently. However, once such a person is elevated to a position of leadership, they tend to do the same thing as the people they criticized. Why? If one is not careful, a proud spirit may enter.

Lust, power, and greed are three powerful spirits that aim to steal from the leader in any organization and to kill and destroy the reputation and headship of that person (John 10:10). This would make the body dysfunctional because we are all one body with one head. The body cannot function unless the head is intact. Therefore, the aim of the enemy is always to try to destroy the head of every organization. It is important that each head, whether it is the head of a local auxiliary, a local church, several churches, multiple churches, or an international ministry, realize that the enemy aims for the head.

A person in leadership must be consecrated and dedicated to the Lord, aware of the subtlety of the enemy and his devices, and understanding his tricks. Sometimes what one feels is a small thing—a smile, a gesture, or a man walking into a forbidden area—but it can cause traumatic damage to the body. The leader should always exercise caution. A person who is offered a position of leadership should carefully consider if he is really willing to pay the cost to be in that position. Is the cost too great? Does he have the stamina and perseverance to hold on and to stand, no matter what comes or goes?

Pride is a spirit that takes control of many leaders. When this happens, they are embarrassed to admit their failures, deficiencies, faults, and weaknesses. Therefore, they do not seek help, and the problems become worse and worse. Embarrassment, shame, discouragement, and depression come, and before you know it, you have a defeated leader. The world tends to look at such a leader as someone who has failed alone, but in actuality, the whole body fails when the leader fails. Therefore, it is important that we always pray for the leaders of organizations so that they may be led and directed by the Spirit of Christ, by the Holy Spirit who dwells within them.

Many leaders who would not be tempted by lust or pride have problems with greed and control. To demand control is to say, "You do what I say. I am in control." It means that a leader, instead of allowing people to follow what is being said, becomes a dictator and begins to retaliate when those who are under his authority begin to question if something should be done another way. The spirit of control causes a leader to try to annihilate one who disagrees with him, and it must be fought with immediate prayer.

I remember an instance when the spirit of control prevented a woman from receiving healing for a health problem that made her unable to walk. She had seen many physicians, but none of them could help her. And because she was a leader of the women in her local church, she only wanted someone of her spiritual stature to pray for her. The Lord had instructed one of His prayer servants to pray for this woman, but He told her not to do it until the woman asked her.

God told the prayer servant, "She has an affliction, not a true sickness, and only obedience can remove this illness. Nothing will make her better, for this was allowed because she touched an anointed vessel of the Lord. Not only did she lie about her but also purposely tried to destroy her character for fear that she would be advanced. Therefore this disease has come upon her. She has further developed the 'I am' syndrome of walking in a prideful and self-righteous state. These people say, 'I am important, I am the only one who can and most of all I give all the glory to the Lord.' In their hearts, they are saying, 'I am the one in control of this situation.'"

We may be tempted to believe that a leader who fasts and prays is exempt from the attacks of the enemy and will not succumb to the enemy's devices. However, even after Elijah fasted and prayed forty days and forty nights, he was full of himself when he answered the Lord's question about what he was doing. He was having a pity party because he felt that he and he alone had the revelation of who God was. He felt that he and he alone was serving God (1 Kings 19:8–10). He did not yet understand what God would yet show him in verse 18, that God had seven thousand who had not bowed the knee to Baal.

When we look around and feel that we are so righteous and that no one else is righteous, it means that we are self-righteous; the spirit of superiority and self-righteousness has taken over our lives. We must be careful that we do not allow this. A leader in spiritual hierarchy must honor even the baby Christians—those who come in and feel that they know it all, and those who feel that they know nothing. He must be cautious and carefully teach and instruct them in the Word of God so that they may be powerful in spiritual warfare.

How Leaders Can Defeat the Works of the Enemy

As we progress up the ladder in leadership, we need teaching so that we know what to expect and what not to expect from the forces of the enemy. We need understanding so that we will not live in fear, but with a mind dedicated to the Lord to live uprightly, to walk uprightly, and to serve Him daily. No matter how high we are in the hierarchy of authority, we have a weak spot, a Goliath spot, for which the enemy searches. If that spot is left uncovered, the enemy will subdue us.

After Jesus was led into the wilderness and fasted forty days and forty nights, He was tempted with everything imaginable, including riches, control, and power. If Jesus was tempted this way, how much more will we, as children of God who possess the Holy Spirit, be tempted as we go up the ladder in our spiritual walk? We must do what Jesus did and use the Word of God, not carnal words or deeds, to fight our battles. This is the only way we can defeat the works of the enemy.

Matthew 4:4 records Jesus' answer to the enemy's first temptation: "It is written, Man shall not live by bread alone, but by every word that proceedeth out of the mouth of God." Did the enemy leave him alone? No, the devil kept going with another temptation. Jesus had to come back in verse 7, "It is written again, Thou shalt not tempt the Lord thy God." Did Satan give up? No, he continued with yet another temptation. So, in verse 10, Jesus had to say, "Get thee hence, Satan: for it is written, Thou shalt worship the Lord thy God, and him only shalt thou serve." And then, in verse 11, the devil left him and "angels came and ministered unto him."

We do battle with a set of demons at every level of our relationship with Christ and the leadership He has entrusted to us. At one level, we may only experience little imps, small things that will upset us. As we climb the ladder, greater demons will come after us—and greater angels will come to minister on our behalf. If we hold on to God through the attack, ministering angels will come to us, just as they did to Jesus.

God is able to give victory over the enemy's attacks against spiritual hierarchy. Six boys who grew up together had many relatives in leadership positions in the same organization, and they all aspired to be the president of the organization. They grew and served, and one by one each had a chance to be the head of the organization. However, each one who reached the top began to behave in a similar manner; they forgot the friendships they once had and were dictatorial in their leadership. Each of them vowed that if he ever got into the leadership position, he would never do what the other ones did, but the same actions took place over and over.

Essentially the same sets of demons were allowed to possess each of the men when they took over the leadership position, and this affected the body of the organization, even though it was a spiritual corporation. However, when one of the men became the leader, he saw what the devil was doing. As he prayed and fasted and sought the Lord daily, the cycle was broken.

It is possible, as John 12:40 says, for our eyes to be blinded to our actions so that we cannot see. If we actually see the wrong we are doing, we will correct it because we would not purposely try to sabotage ourselves or the body of Christ. Many are blinded because of evil spirits and are not willing to yield to correction because they feel they have to be right if they are in a position of authority. They think that they should not take advice or counsel from someone who is not in their position. As they stumble over and over again, others around them see what they are unable to see in themselves. Ongoing prayer, fasting, and consecration to God is required for those in leadership to be victorious over evil and lead the people of the Lord in His provision of victory.

I have noticed that spirits of jealousy, envy, and striving have attacked those who serve on the level of a lay teacher and a Sunday School teacher. As a teacher is elevated to director of a particular department, stronger spirits—lust and power—could come and attempt to defeat that person. If one advances further to assistant pastor and even to pastor and higher, greater spirits of lust, power, greed, and control may attempt to overtake and overshadow.

The prayers of the righteous avail much for one who is in leadership; therefore, it is imperative that we pray for those in leadership positions. There should be intercessory prayer for leadership not one day, but daily. People in leadership should also take time for rest, for recreation, for personal time, and for exercise. This is extremely important, because one who is tired is much more likely to succumb to evil spirits than one who is physically fit and prayed up. Tiredness and stress cause one to make mistakes in judgment. Under these circumstances, the wisdom of the Lord is distorted, and one's disobedience results in the entry of evil spirits.

A person in leadership must take care of himself for the sake of the body as a whole. This is very important because strength is necessary to win our spiritual battles. As long as Aaron and Hur held up Moses' hands, the children of Israel prevailed (Exod. 17:12), but when his arms were let down, the children of Israel began to suffer defeat. It is important that we hold up the hands and arms of those in leadership with prayer, kindness, and encouragement. It will help them succeed in their God-given work, and it will help the growth of the body of Christ.

The next time you see a failure in leadership, don't be so quick to criticize or to analyze. Instead, learn to pray and intercede for that one who has fallen. If you feel that you are strong, remember that it is possible for you, the one who is judging, to be overtaken in that same fault. It may take a week, a month, a year, or several years, but one day you may be in that position. Take heed and pray for one another. Love one another, and pray especially for those in leadership positions. Galatians 6:1 states, "Brethren, if a man be overtaken in a fault, ye which are spiritual, restore such an one in the spirit of meekness; considering thyself, lest thou also be tempted."

PART II

SPIRITS IN THE ENEMY'S EMPLOY

4

LUST

Now the works of the flesh are manifest, which are these; Adultery, fornication, uncleanness, lasciviousness.

Galatians 5:19

The apostle Paul began his list of the works of the flesh with various expressions of sexual sin—adultery, fornication, uncleanness, and lasciviousness—that have their root in lust. *Webster's Collegiate Dictionary* defines *lust* as "pleasure, delight, to have an intense desire to need; crave; to have a sexual urge." According to the Bible, lust is considered an evil desire. Many think of lust only as a sexual desire, but it can be expressed in many forms and in many ways. Anything craving or any desire that drives a person to be wanton leads to lust. One can lust after power, food, men, women, control or even a particular car. Lust is an overwhelming desire for something.

From the beginning, the devil conceived in his heart to overthrow the throne and kingdom of God. He, along with the angels that followed him, exalted himself against God and His power because lust for power was conceived in his heart. It was borne in him that he wanted to be greater than the Lord God. The apostle John described this when he wrote:

> He that committeth sin is of the devil; for the devil sinneth from the beginning. For this purpose the Son of God was manifested, that he might destroy the works of the devil. Whosoever is born of God doth not commit sin; for his seed remaineth in him: and he cannot sin, because he is born of God.
>
> —1 John 3:8–9

One who is not born of God sins and continues in sin over and over again without repentance, remorse, contriteness of the heart, and brokenness of the spirit. He does not have the seed of God in him in the form of the Holy Spirit. However, if one is born of God, the seed of God remains in him. This is not to say, especially for a young believer, that a Christian does not make a mistake and sin; it does mean that he does not continue to do those things that he knows are wrong. There is a point at which one recognizes his sin and emerges from it with true repentance.

Once the seed of God is planted within the heart of a believer, it grows and grows. As it grows, the manifestation becomes evident in the form of righteous living, not only to the believer, but also to those around him. The things that are inside our hearts and minds are the things that we perform. As we allow them to linger and grow in magnitude in our hearts and minds, we do them.

This principle helps explain why we do things that are unrighteous. In Matthew 15:19, Jesus said, "For out of the heart proceed evil thoughts, murders, adulteries, fornications, thefts, false witness, blasphemies." If we do not rebuke evil thoughts and repent of them, they will grow day-in and day-out until they are no longer controllable. Good thought will summon an angel to work on one's behalf, but craving and lust will take on demonic force.

But, as James teaches, it all starts in the heart and mind of a person:

> But every man is tempted, when he is drawn away of his own lust, and enticed. Then when lust hath conceived, it bringeth forth sin: and sin, when it is finished, bringeth forth death.
>
> —James 1:14–15

If we allow a lustful thought to linger in our mind, it tempts us—entices and draws us—to be more and more interested in that than in the things of the Lord and His Word. As we lose our focus on the Lord, we lose our strength and power in Christ and become weaker and weaker to the desires of our flesh. We become open and susceptible to the power of evil. This is why we commit the actual act of sin.

An excellent analogy is what happens after the sperm and the egg unite to form a zygote during conception. If the zygote is allowed to live and grow in the uterine wall, it will produce a fetus. However, if it is implanted in the fallopian tubes, problems will arise because they usually are not able to sustain the weight of the fetus. Bleeding will occur, and the mother could even die if she does not receive the necessary help. Sometimes the tube has to be completely removed, and other times one can simply take out the fertilized egg and reattach the tubes to make them functional. Scarring occurs, and if one tube is taken out, only one tube is functional for childbearing.

When a lustful thought is conceived, we must deal with it thoroughly. It must be cleansed and removed so that there is no scarring, no residue, no entrapment for further conceptions of it. The Word of God clearly teaches us that God does not entice us or entangle us. Rather our thinking, our thought process, and our focus cause us to drift from righteous living into evil.

The Dangers of Lust

The apostle Paul warned us about the dangers of lust in his first letter to Timothy:

> But those who crave to be rich fall into temptation and a snare and into many foolish (useless, godless) and hurtful desires that plunge men into ruin and destruction and miserable perishing. For the love of money is a root of all evils; it is through this craving that some have been led astray and have

wandered from the faith and pierced themselves through with many acute [mental] pangs.

—1 Timothy 6:9–10, amp

A pang is torment. It can be a brief, piercing spasm of pain or even a sharp attack of mental anguish that happens as a result of our efforts to be happy. We go from one thing to another, seeking joy and happiness in sources such as traveling, fancy cars, big houses, beautiful jets, and beautiful clothing. We may try to find happiness in alcohol, drugs, and multiple affairs. Yet, in all our efforts, we are not content or happy but tormented instead.

Relationships with family members and friends cannot be bought. Even though one may have a large house, that does not make it a home. A husband can buy a large diamond ring for his wife, and a wife can buy expensive clothes for her husband, but that does not make a marriage. Happiness cannot be bought, and neither can it be acquired by elevation to a desired position.

True happiness, true pleasure, comes only from a relationship with the Lord. It is true that Ecclesiastes tells us that "money answereth all things" (Eccles. 10:19). Money pays bills and buys clothing and cars, but we must be careful that we do not lust or crave to be rich. It will cause much anguish and even stress to the body, which promotes an increase in acidic flow in the gastrointestinal tract and possibly even irritation in the stomach and other parts of the intestine. This will result in an ulcer or possibly other physical abnormalities, such as high blood pressure, which may further lead to a stroke, a heart attack, and other issues that would not normally occur in the absence of such stress.

I am not suggesting that riches should not be sought or obtained, but I do maintain that it should be done in a lawful way. Abraham, according to the Word of God, was very rich, but he obeyed God and his faith was counted as righteousness. Even when Abraham messed up and said that Sarah was his sister instead of his wife, God blessed him and caused men to give unto his bosom because He loved him and had a covenant with him (Gen. 12; Rom. 4:1–12).

Lust, after it has been given expression, leads to lasciviousness, unbridled lust. Paul described this in his second letter to Timothy:

> For among them are those who worm their way into homes and captivate silly and weak-natured and spiritually dwarfed women, loaded down with [the burden of their] sins [and easily] swayed and led away by various evil desires and seductive impulses. [These weak women will listen to anybody who will teach them]; they are forever inquiring and getting information, but are never able to arrive at a recognition and knowledge of the Truth.
>
> —2 Timothy 3:6–7, AMP

Many feel that they have no hope because they are so weak and burdened by their life situations. Because they are looking so desperately for relief, they are open to things that they may know are not right. They desire what feels good, even though it brings hurt, shame, and pain to them. This is not to belittle the feelings of anyone, nor to suggest that burdens and pains are easy to carry. Some have strengths that others do not have.

However, the strong are to help those who are weaker by offering prayer and supplication for them. We are not to condemn others, but we are commanded to tell one another the truth in love (Eph. 4:15). We are to point each other not to ourselves or to any person, but to the eternal source, who has strength, power, and knowledge for us all. We receive hope and strength through the Word of God and through the blood of Jesus that was shed on the cross.

Lustful, lascivious acts do not go unpunished. According to Romans 1:24–32, those that commit such deeds are eventually turned over to their uncleanness. The Lord allows the limits to be taken off of their cravings and desires so that they go, essentially, into a rage and commit sinful acts uncontrollably until they either repent or reach the place where they are consumed. No one can tame or harness their acts, and they are essentially driven day in and day out by their craving and urgings. They are never satisfied by their indulgence in a sexual act, acts of greed, gluttony, gossip, or control.

Nothing is shameful to those who are lascivious. This goes for sexual lust, which this chapter will particularly discuss, and also for backbiters, slanderers, and those who appear to have no conscience, no heart for anyone, no mercy, and no love. Romans 1:32 says, "Though they are fully aware of God's righteous decree that those who do such things deserve to die, they not only do them themselves but approve and applaud others who practice them" (AMP). Those who have been turned over to a lasciviousness not only participate actively in what they feel is their right to do; they also tell others it is OK to do it and thereby cause them to fall into the same snares.

The Cost of Lasciviousness

Acts of lust and lasciviousness—one name for them is *indecency*—often manifest in the lives of those who come from a background of dysfunctional relationships. One man who grew up in a dysfunctional family married a beautiful young lady and earned a PhD. Even though his wife was available for his enjoyment, something inside him caused him to seek affirmation from other women. Even when his wife was planning to come on a work trip with him, anytime she was not there, he would quickly grab another woman to spend the night with and then wait for his wife.

After several years of marriage, his wife learned about his various affairs when she caught him in a lie. She was five to six months pregnant at the time and drove off in the middle of a storm because she was so upset. She had a terrible car accident and was hospitalized for an extended period of time. The baby survived, although it was born prematurely and had multiple defects. And though the husband asked for forgiveness, the marriage was very, very rocky.

Another man, who received no affection from his parents, began to molest other children, even relatives, when he was a child. He had multiple relationships as an adult, both before and after he finally married. He raped a young lady who was obtaining money from him and was eventually jailed for stealing and for writing bad checks.

In yet another story, a young lady was molested by her father for approximately nine years, beginning when she was a little girl. He threatened to kill her, her mother, and the rest of the family if she told, and she was so distraught that she felt she would lose her mind. She became very promiscuous in school, thinking that she might get pregnant to cover for what her father was doing. She then sought the attention of boys who would abuse her, and she began to do drugs before the age of fifteen.

Even though she attempted to tell adults about her father's deeds, they would not believe her. Finally, she got the attention of her mother, who knew nothing of what was going on. When her mother confronted the father, he admitted to his lascivious acts and left. The young lady wanted to commit suicide because she felt that she was at fault for what had happened. However, because of prayer and intercession, she became a powerful teaching model for others who were abused.

A person who has a lustful demon is consumed by lust not because his sex drive has increased, but because evil spirits are driving him. When lust is conceived in a sexual way, many times the acts performed become more varied and more intense because the human spirit within is trying to be satisfied. Many even seek to have orgies or multiple partners at one time, thinking it will satisfy. However, nothing does satisfy because there has to be more, more, more. The answer to life problems such as these is the Word of God. It is reaching the Lord and touching Him. Yet, it is not done as easily as it is said, for God's powerful work of deliverance is required.

When a husband or wife is driven by lust to be unfaithful

to his or her mate, he or she may quickly stop the sinful relationship when God reveals that it is wrong. Even when this happens, however, the marriage suffers great damage. For instance, a young lady became pregnant from an affair, and she and her husband raised the child as her husband's child because he did not know that the child was not his. However, when a blood test had to be made for a transfusion, the husband discovered that the child that he had raised as his own was actually another man's son. It destroyed the marriage.

Extramarital relationships such as the one I have just described are much too common. According to Masters and Johnson, nearly 50 percent of married women and close to 70 percent of married men have extramarital relationships.[1] In 1 Corinthians 6:18, the Bible explains that there is a cost for each of these relationships. Because the sins of adultery and fornication are done in the body but affect the spirit, the two participating people are joined together and become one flesh. When this happens, the spirit of the extramarital partner somewhat remains with the married person if repentance and cleansing does not take place.

Therefore, a person who has sexual intercourse with one who has been sexually involved with other partners is actually engaging with all those partners, all those spirits, which tend to remain unless true repentance comes. It is scary to think about, but what if you join with a person who has been with ten people who may have also been with at least three people? If you use the multiplying power, you could end up sleeping with thirty people or more, dealing with each one of those spirits, without even knowing it.

We must be careful what we do. Romans 6:23 reminds us that the wages, the payment, for sin is death. It is not only physical death, but also, if one rejects Christ, spiritual death. It may be marital death, and sometimes it causes a breakdown in one's mental ability. We must consider the choices we make about allowing lust to take over our mind and rob us of control over our urges and cravings and the place we express them. If we do not, demonic control can result in public and private acts of lasciviousness.

Many believe that once we come into salvation our sins are cast into the sea of forgetfulness and remembered no more. While this is true, our sins are actions that result in costly, painful repercussions we may experience many years after we have given our lives to Christ. Sexual pleasure for a season, for a moment, for an instant, may cause a lifetime of pain and agony. Fornication and adultery cause terrible disruption because they not only affect the two people involved, but also families and the future of many generations. We must guard our spiritual walk with the Lord, and as 1 Corinthians 6:18 warns, "Flee fornication."

Lust Destroys, but God Delivers

As we have seen, lust, in any form, is dangerous, but sexual lust can destroy. History tells that Napoleon Bonaparte was a powerful ruler who had multiple affairs, and as a result, died of a venereal disease. He was driven by lust to conquer the world, and he also had a lust for women. He had to pay the price for both lusts.

William Shakespeare wrote many wonderful pieces that the

world has enjoyed for many years. In one of his writings, *Lewd Lexicon...Act of Darkness...Bone Ache, Due to Pain of Venereal Disease*, he described the hurt and pain of this disease in such exquisite detail that it suggests he had some personal knowledge of it. Shakespeare died of an unknown disease at the age of fifty-two, and in his will, he left a large portion of his inheritance to a woman who was not his wife and also to the woman's daughter.[2] Perhaps the author did engage in lustful acts.

Throughout history, many celebrities have died of venereal diseases at an early age. Lives that had meaning, lives that were needed to impact the future of others, were shortened by the spirit of sexual lust. Lives that could have been preserved were ended because lust had consumed them. To be bound by the spirit of lust is to be tormented. Lust demands that it be fed and cared for *right now*. It demands that the person, the body it occupies, be prostituted for its needs. The body will do whatever the spirit of lust tells it to do because the craving must be satisfied.

This is what happened when a man who loved the Lord and preached His Word overextended himself in his ministry and prayer for many people. Because he did not spend time with the Lord and listen to Him, he reached a state of near exhaustion and began to have extramarital affairs, which led to a life of lasciviousness. Although multiple people trusted him and looked to him for guidance, he also began to have relationships with teenage boys. The boys were very angry, but they were afraid to tell anyone because they felt people would not believe them. The man, along with many of the teens he violated, ended up with AIDS and died with the disease, even though the man repented and asked others to forgive him before he left this world.

God's deliverance from lasciviousness is illustrated in the story of two young ladies who were rejected by their fathers and also mistreated by every young man they tried to date. They began to have multiple relationships with both men and with women and forsook the biblical teaching that warned against homosexual relationships (Lev. 18:22; Rom. 1:26–27). The two young ladies continued in their bisexual acts until one went exclusively to homosexual relationships. However, by God's grace and delivering power, they decided to give their lives to the Lord and became heterosexual again.

In another instance, a boy who had lived a sheltered life grew into a pattern of lasciviousness that was marked by multiple sexual relationships and orgies. Even though he married a young woman whom he loved very much, he continued to have relationships with other women, both married and single. If a lady even suggested that she was interested in him, he would find where she lived and force himself on her. Because of his lustful actions, he was arrested by the police many times, until he, after many years of this behavior, decided to give his life to the Lord. When he did, he received deliverance, full and clear.

One young woman grew up in a home in which her mother loved the Lord, but the father had never given his life wholly to the Lord. The mother fussed and argued and was verbally abusive to the children, while the father, though he was loving, had multiple affairs. All the children—three sons and one daughter—followed the pattern of their father. The daughter was essentially promiscuous with anyone who desired her, and she got to the point that she was sure she was HIV-positive. This sent her on a rampage of infecting as many people she possibly could, only to find out that she was not HIV-positive.

As she continued her lascivious lifestyle, she entered a ministry with the purpose of finding men, married and single, who looked lonely. If they looked as if their wives were not caring for them, her mission was to sleep with every one of them. However, instead of succeeding in this, she was shown love and kindness and found that she could no longer do what she was doing. No matter how bad she acted, she was loved and treated with kindness. As a result, she gave her life to the Lord.

Shortly after this, she found a mate who loved the Lord and was dedicated to Him. He treated her like a queen, and they gave their lives to minister together. Because of the things she had encountered as a youth with her parents, she had problems, even after they were married. In fact, it was only after several years of spiritual counseling that she emerged as the person the Lord intended her to be. She had many defeats and hurts that surfaced in her new life with her husband, but she was able to conquer them through the blood of Jesus and through her faith in the Lord.

5

IDOLATRY AND WITCHCRAFT

Now the works of the flesh are manifest, which are these; Adultery, fornication, uncleanness, lasciviousness, Idolatry, witchcraft.

GALATIANS 5:19–20, EMPHASIS ADDED

IDOLATRY IS THE worship of idols, gods, or even a devotion to or blind or excessive adoration. Idols—gods of gold, gods of silver, graven images—were worshiped in many instances in the Bible, even though God strongly forbade it:

> I am the LORD thy God, which have brought thee out of the land of Egypt, out of the house of bondage. Thou shalt have no other gods before me. Thou shalt not make unto thee any graven image, or any likeness of any thing that is in heaven above, or that is in the earth beneath, or that is in the

> water under the earth. Thou shalt not bow down thyself to them, nor serve them: for I the Lord thy God am a jealous God, visiting the iniquity of the fathers upon the children unto the third and fourth generation of them that hate me.
>
> —Exodus 20:2–5

Almighty God said that we are not to create an image to bow down to in worship or to serve in the place of Him. In Exodus 22:20 He further warned, "He that sacrificeth unto any god, save unto the Lord only, he shall be utterly destroyed." Sadly, while Moses was on Mount Sinai receiving instructions for building the tabernacle, Aaron was persuaded by the children of Israel to make them graven images, a golden calf that they could worship as a god. Therefore, in Exodus 32:7, the Lord spoke to Moses and told him to get down quickly from the mount because the people had corrupted themselves. The Lord was angry with them, but Moses interceded for them and asked Him to forgive their sin.

Some centuries later, when Solomon was king of Israel, his heart was turned from the Lord to idols. God was angry because He had twice warned Solomon not to follow after other gods, nor to marry strange women. Solomon did the opposite, and therefore felt for a while that everything was empty and vanity. Although his heart eventually returned to the Lord, idol worship tragically took him from the presence of the Lord for a time.

Idol worship extends beyond the action of bowing before physical objects that human hands have formed to be objects of worship. It also extends to cars, houses, diamonds and riches, anything we put above God. Our husband, our wife, and our children can be idols. There is nothing more sacred than our relationship with the Lord. Therefore, anything that we put before the Lord—even our thoughts and desires—becomes an idol.

Examples of Idolatry

A woman who was the head of an organization worshiped not only her position, but also the attention, honor, and praise she received. Everyone respected her, and when she walked into the room, everyone would automatically stand. She ruled the organization with an iron fist, and it became her god to the extent that she gave her whole life to build it. She did not even marry and have children. When the organization declined and then closed, the woman died not of natural causes but because she had nothing else to live for. The thing that she had worshiped as god had left her.

For another woman, her whole life had become the corporation in which she held a position. When she was lying on her deathbed, she felt that she was that corporation and that the corporation could not go on without her. She had made an idol out of the thing that she was simply a part of. After her death, the corporation continued and flourished even more because the person who filled her position allowed individuals to excel according to their abilities rather than through personal favors they did.

When we talk about idolatry, we may look back at the Aztecs on the eve of the Spanish conquest in the sixteenth century. According to Jacques Soustelle, many sacrifices were made, and many dances were performed. Some considered the dances beautiful, others considered them terrible rituals, and yet others considered them horrifying. Some people even danced in human skin the evening before the rituals, sacrificing to their gods.[1]

Those who were of the Texcoco tribe were so religious that it is impossible to know how many gods they honored. Native Americans have always practiced rituals of service to false gods. Some of them say, "We do not ask the white man to do as the Indian, but we choose to continue in our native rituals, while many have converted to Christianity."[2]

Witchcraft idolatry is very real even today in many cultures. In an Indian ritual that entices evil spirits, Kwakiutl winter dances tell of long ago when spirits roamed the earth in human form. As hunters trekked deep into the forest in search of mountain goats, they suddenly heard an eerie whistling sound. A giant, who was supposedly a cannibal, came in, his eyes gleaming hungrily. He had a team of carnivorous birds who cracked open skulls to eat human brains and ravens who plucked out the eyes.[3]

Together these birds represented the darkest forces of uncontrolled human desires. The hunters escaped with their lives, but they also took with them the secrets of the cannibal's power, including the masks, whistles, cedar bark, apron dances, and apron songs. Back in the village they reenacted the whole ordeal, causing horror to some and delight to others. They also represented figures that embodied both good and evil.

In 1989, Hopi elder Mike Gashwazra saw a mask that had

been stolen from an Indian tribe and was now in a museum. It was a thirty-nine-inch yucca-fiber disk covered by deer skin, painted with green, red, black, and white pigments, and topped with a crown of braided corn husks and feathers. As the Indian priest saw the mask, he immediately took out corn and began to put it on top of the mask in an attempt to feed what he identified as "the spirits." He murmured, "You have your god."[4]

Many believe in idols and false gods today, not only those we see in our day-to-day life, but also in statues, in gold and silver, and in the worship of spirits and inanimate objects. This is very real today in many cultures in America and in other countries. It is definitely not obsolete.

The Spirit of Witchcraft

As we have seen in the section above, the spirit of idolatry is related to the spirit of witchcraft. The Internet lists hundreds of Web sites for witchcraft, and it also provides access to formal training for one who decides to try witchcraft. The practice of witchcraft, which may also be called sorcery, occurs in many countries. For instance, when a young man in an African nation broke his leg, the witch doctor took a chicken and broke the chicken's leg in the same place the young man's leg was broken. In a matter of about three days, the chicken was miraculously healed, as well as the young man.

During a conference at one of the islands in the United States, I recognized the presence of a spirit of witchcraft in my hotel suite. I turned the television off, and it went off. However, as I lay on my bed, it came back on a few minutes later. I turned it off again, and it turned itself back on. Finally, I got up and turned it off and stood there. Even though it did not come back on, voices started coming through the television set and things in the room began to move. I rebuked it in the name of Jesus, and everything stopped. There was no more movement.

When I was a young believer, I went to my uncle-in-law's church, and he informed my husband and me that there were people who practiced witchcraft in that setting. He said several women in the church were practicing witches, who had been observing the church and had even become participants in the congregation. He advised us, especially me, not to touch any of them as we were ministering that day. He said that we were praying and the blood of Jesus would sustain the ministry and the people. Yet, he warned that we should not go and lay hands on them.

At the end of service, we were asked to join hands with the person next to us. One of the women who was practicing witchcraft was watching me, and I moved far away from her. However, she moved all the way around in the circle and extended her hand to me. The Lord spoke to me and said, "Go ahead." When she touched me I could feel a small current in my fingertips and the Lord said, "Hold on." As I held on and grabbed her hand with full force, she quickly removed her hand from mine, began to shake her whole arm, and ran away. The Lord encouraged me with the words, "The Spirit of the Lord is far greater than any witchcraft. The Holy Spirit in you and in believers, and in saints, and in Christians, is much greater than any witchcraft spirit. Use the power that is within you."

A woman approximately seventy-years-old had no fibroids, but had the stomach of a nine-month pregnancy. There was no pregnancy, no baby, and there were no tumors. But every night she would, essentially, go through labor pains and the motion of pushing a baby out of her stomach. She went from physician to physician looking for an answer for this, but could find none. Finally, it was discovered that someone had given her a potion. After prayer and deliverance, she was freed from this.

In another instance of witchcraft that occurred in 2002, a young lady who wanted a husband went to a practicing witch and received a potion to put in her boyfriend's cup. When this potion was put in his cup, it caused the young man to essentially run after her and desire only her. However, she would have to continually put potions in his cup if she wanted to keep him. After receiving wise counsel, she realized she really did not want a man whom she had to trick for the rest of her life, and she also understood that the Lord was not pleased with such actions. She stopped giving him the potion, and less than a year later the Lord blessed her with a great husband who loves Him and her.

As we consider these stories we must be wise as serpents, but meek as doves. We must also realize that the Lord will protect us if we are not knowledgeable of the things we are ingesting. However, if wisdom exists, we must be careful about the things we take into our body. We must know those who labor among us, those who are serving us, and those who are our cup-bearers. We must know the people around us and those who say that they love us, not being paranoid, but understanding that spirits and witchcraft are very real.

In 1 Samuel 15, God, through Samuel, commanded King Saul to totally destroy the Amalekites and all their property. When Saul did not fully obey this command, Samuel confronted him and said:

> And Samuel said, Hath the LORD as great delight in burnt offerings and sacrifices, as in obeying the voice of the LORD? Behold, to obey is better than sacrifice, and to hearken than the fat of rams. For rebellion is as the sin of witchcraft, and stubbornness is as iniquity and idolatry. Because thou hast rejected the word of the LORD, he hath also rejected thee from being king.
>
> —1 SAMUEL 15:22–23

God was very displeased with Saul and said that his lack of complete obedience was an act of rebellion that warranted his removal from being king. Saul, in effect, had said, "I exalt my opinion over your opinion. I exalt my thoughts over your thoughts." His actions had in actuality been as the spirit of witchcraft because they expressed his self-will, high-mindedness, and pride.

MEDIEVAL ROOTS OF WITCHCRAFT[5]

The word *witch* comes from the Anglo-Saxon word *wicce*. It was derived from an Indo-European root word that means "to bend or change" or "to do magical things" along with religion. It is related to the words *wicker, wiggle,* and even *vicar.* A woman who practices witchcraft is referred to as witch, while a male who does the same is referred to as a warlock.

In medieval Europe, ordinary folks everywhere believed in the supernatural and the existence of spirits, including demons, imps, and legendary creatures such as vampires, werewolves, and even unicorns. Magic was considered as powerful as prayer, and the kingdom of darkness with its devils and evil spirits was understood to be very real. As the Renaissance came to Europe, superstitions were strong, if not stronger than they had ever been in earlier generations. Even the writing of William Shakespeare (1564–1666) was full of illusion, magic, and witches.

Soothsayers and wizards were people who foretold things to come and raised up evil spirits by certain superstitious and conceived forms of words. Diviners, professors of the art of divination, were puffed up with prophesying spirits. Jugglers were flighty curers of all manner of diseases and sores of man and beast. Enchanters and charmers used words and images and herbs to perform supernatural acts.

Witches were considered to be hags who had made a pact with the devil through his persuasion, inspiration, and thought. They could bring about all manner of evil things, either by thought or imprecation, by means such as shaking the air with lightning and thunder and by causing hail and tempests. Witches were believed to be carried by familiar spirits, which had taken upon them the shape of a goat, swine, or calf. They were said to sometimes fly upon a staff or fork or some other instrument and to spend all the night with a sweetheart, playing, sporting, bantering, dancing, and doing diverse activities of devilish lust.

Trials intended to punish practitioners of witchcraft because it was against the law of God began in England and in Scotland in the 1500s. These efforts were a warning to many people, including men of scholarship and learning who believed in witchcraft. In 1608, a ninety-year-old priest cut his throat to avoid being burned as a warlock and suffered the horrors of total demonic possession in his death.

After a while, everyone who looked like a hag, perhaps because they suffered from a physical disease or were elderly, was suspected to be a witch. One lady who was not a witch said that she, because of the continual gossip about her, was forced to become a witch:

> And why on me? Why should the envious world throw all their scandalous malice upon me? 'Cause I am poor, deformed and ignorant, and like a bow buckled and bent together, by some more strong and mischievous than myself? Must I for that be made a common sink, for all the filth and rubbish of men's tongue to fall and run into? Some call me witch; and being ignorant of myself, they go about to teach me how to be one: urging that my bad tongue (by their uses made so) for speaks their cattle, doeth bewitch their corn, themselves, their servant, and their babes at nurse. This they enforce upon me: and in part make me to credit it.[6]

Some believed that those who were witches had marks that the devil forced them to take, a stamp that showed they belonged to him. A Scottish witch named Isobel Gowdie described something like this in 1662 when she confessed that she made a pact with the devil. She said that she met with the devil more than once and that he sometimes appeared as a deer or a roe. Sometimes he wore boots and sometimes he wore shoes, but his feet were forked and cloven.

According to Arthur Guazzo, witchcraft is an inherited power passed down from one generation to the next.[7] Many witches have admitted that the things they practice have been passed down from their parents to them. In confessions they made at witch trials all over Germany, France, Scotland, and England, witches said that they had to prick their fingers and sacrifice blood so the witchcraft would work.

A Word More Powerful Than Witchcraft

In his book, Dr. Ken Olson has described witchcraft as the lust for power.[8] He has said there has never before been such an increasing evidence of the occult in bookstores; music, such as heavy metal, black metal, and rock; and witchcraft, New Age, and Satan worship. People are fascinated by the abundance of demonic movies, television shows, and even Saturday morning cartoons that glorify and fantasize the very demons of hell.

However, the demonic realm is not just a fantasy, a cartoon world to be played with. Rather, it is a world with subtle snares that will draw people in to a place they are not ready for, a place of being possessed by evil spirits. The thing about the seduction of the devil is that it always leads to "self destruction." Witchcraft, Ouija boards, and black magic are nothing to play with. Some, according to Roger Hart, have gone as far as participating in human sacrifices and cannibalism.[9] Yes, witchcraft is something to be avoided.

As we have seen, witchcraft has been an instrument of much evil throughout the world. Witches have used sorcery and black magic to bewitch men—seduce, control, and maneuver them—to be their "sexual slaves." This happened to my grandfather in his early twenties. At the insistence of my grandmother, who was also young at the time, he tried to be helpful to an older woman who lived next door. The woman used witchcraft when she prepared coffee for him to drink, and he left my grandmother, who was young and very attractive, for the older lady. When my grandfather learned what the older lady was doing, he left her, even though it was hard.

Although the enemy is very active through witchcraft, Christ gives us victory over him. This is what happened as a result of prayer for a stroke victim who had been unfaithful to his wife. For no medical reason, he went in and out of reality, and the Lord allowed our prayer team to see that it was because of witchcraft. When we spoke to his mother about this, she told us that he had been with a woman who practiced witchcraft.

After we prayed for the man and were assured that he had been released from the spell, we went into the hallway. Just then, the lady he had been with stepped off the elevator, and, even though I had never seen her before, I knew it was her. The lady took one look at me, and quickly got back onto the elevator because she recognized the spirit of Christ in me. She retreated quickly according to the witches' creed. Within three days, the man went home with a clear mind. He was told not to go back to that lady again.

In May 2004 a woman came to my office and told me of the evil influence of witchcraft through an affair she had with a man who was much older than her. When she was with him one day she noticed a very foul odor that could not be traced to any natural causes. The scent continued when he would visit her house and strange things began to happen. Instead of sleeping in the bed with her he would sleep in her walk-in closet and would stand on the kitchen counter for hours. The smell would be deposited wherever he was.

When the man began to put a white chemical—it was not cocaine or any drug—up her nose and into her ears, she started to see things come out of her being and walk in the room. The only way she could obtain peace was to find the Twenty-third Psalm in her Bible and place it on her stomach. She finally got the courage to leave the man, but her house still had the odor and she could feel someone choking her at night. She received the prayer of faith and agreed with a believer that she, her house, and her family would be delivered from the power of witchcraft. She anointed the house and herself and was totally delivered through the blood of Jesus.

An ex-witch who came from a line of witches once spoke to me in an interview and told me that her witchcraft was not like that seen on television. It did not consist of a big black pot or brooms, but it was the spoken word that came from her mouth. She mastered the spirit of curses and whatever she said—it was always a curse or something negative—would always come true.

As she explained, the Christian world really does not understand the power of the tongue and our spoken words. In the mist of the darkness in her life, she found a word greater and more powerful than witchcraft and evil. She found Christ and the power of His name, which delivered her from the spirit of witchcraft and brought her to a place where she now speaks blessings upon the children of the Lord.

6

NEGATIVITY, HATRED, AND BITTERNESS

Now the works of the flesh are manifest, which are these; Adultery, fornication, uncleanness, lasciviousness, Idolatry, witchcraft, hatred.

GALATIANS 5:19–20, EMPHASIS ADDED

NEGATIVITY IS SOMETHING we have all experienced at one time or another. The spirit of negativity hinders, binds, and sometimes totally destroys one's vision or destiny. We learn why this spirit, which expresses itself in murmuring and complaining, is so bad from the story of Israel's forty years of wandering in the wilderness.

Exodus 2:24 tells how the Lord heard the cry of the children of Israel after they had suffered four hundred years of slavery in Egypt. Succeeding chapters describe how He struck their oppressors with ten plagues that persuaded Pharaoh to let them go. And because of God's strong hand of deliverance, the Israelites, along with some of the Egyptians, gathered their goods to journey to the land of Canaan.

According to Exodus 13:17–18, they could have traveled by two different routes. They could have gone by the way of the Philistines, which was the shortcut to Canaan, but the Lord did not want fear to overcome them if they saw giants or massive armies. He did not want them to return to the land from which they had been delivered. The other route, which was by the way of the Red Sea, was longer, but even then, it should have only taken about a week.

As the children of Israel came to the Red Sea, they faced the problem of crossing it. They had to make a choice to trust God, or turn back, which would mean slavery again or even death. Their problem grew even more desperate when Pharaoh decided to capture them again and came after them with his army. Moses chose to trust I AM, the One who had sent him to free His people, but before the Lord could perform the miracle the people begin to complain. In Exodus 14:11, they asked Moses, "Because there were no graves in Egypt, hast thou taken us away to die in the wilderness?" Even though God had miraculously delivered them, they were unthankful and had already begun to murmur.

In spite of Israel's negative spirit, the Lord opened the Red Sea for His people to cross it, and He also destroyed the Egyptian army so the people would have no fear or doubt of the total authority He possessed. His sovereignty was undeniable as well as unquestionable. Yet, what should have been the greatest week in the lives of the Israelites turned instead into a forty-year nightmare because of their unbelief and negativity. When the people became thirsty they began to murmur against Moses and ask, "What shall we drink?" (Exod. 15:24).

The Lord lovingly provided sweet water for the children of Israel after Moses obeyed His command to cast a tree into the waters of Marah, which had previously been bitter. God promised the people that no disease of the Egyptians would come upon them if they would listen to Him and do that which was right in His sight and keep His commandments (Exod. 15:26). What a deal! Just love God enough to trust Him and allow Him to provide all that you need in life by merely asking. It required no effort but to ask God instead of complain, to be faithful and serve Him alone as their Lord and God.

God wanted to prove to the children of Israel that He was all they needed. He wanted them to know Him as a Provider and Lord so they would trust Him for all things. When they asked for bread, He provided manna (Exod. 16:14). When they asked for meat, He provided quail. And when they complained and murmured because of their thirst in the wilderness, He gave them water from a rock (Exod. 17:1–7).

Even though the Lord performed miracle after miracle for Israel, the people soon forgot and then began to turn again to their sinful ways. Therefore, God said, "I will change what I had intended for you because you are not ready for the Promised Land if you cannot obey me." As a result, they wandered in the wilderness for forty years.

The Power of the Tongue

The spirit of negativity that plagued the children of Israel did not die with them in the wilderness. It has been a source of evil in every generation, and Jesus spoke strongly against it when He told the Jews to stop murmuring among themselves because of His teaching that He was the Bread that had come down from heaven (John 6:41–43). In Philippians 2:14–15, Paul said that we are to "do all things without murmurings and disputings: That ye may be blameless and harmless, the sons of God, without rebuke, in the midst of a crooked and perverse nation, among whom ye shine as lights in the world."

Jude 14–16 reminds us of Enoch's warning about those who complain and speak negatively about others behind their backs while they give compliments in front of those same people to gain their favor. This is wrong and sinful, and the light and love of the Lord does not shine through us if we do this. If there is no light in us, the only thing others will see is darkness.

Numbers 12 teaches us an important lesson about the consequences of giving in to the spirit of negativity. Verse 1 says that "Miriam and Aaron spake against Moses because of the Ethiopian woman whom he had married: for he had married an Ethiopian woman." This complaint was directed against Moses not only because of the woman he had married, but also because Miriam and Aaron were questioning the God-given authority that had been entrusted to Moses as Israel's leader (v. 2).

The murmuring and complaining of Miriam and Aaron resulted in negative consequences to them individually and also to the others around them. Because of the anger of the Lord against Miriam, she became a leper for seven days. She had to be shut out of the camp during that time, and the whole camp of Israel, with its hundreds of thousands of people, did not move. Miriam held all the people from moving because of her mouth. Because Aaron was still wearing his priestly garments, God did not at this time deal with him for his part in the sin he and Miriam committed. However, the Lord did at a later time ask him to remove his priestly garments before he died (Num. 20:28).

We must be careful that we do not speak words the devil can use as instruments to hinder or even stop the progression of others. Instead, we must learn to give thanks in all things and in all situations so that the Lord may be glorified. (Please read the essay "Negativity and Stress: Sweating the Small Stuff" in Appendix C.) Long after we are gone, our words will continue to live in the minds of others. As Proverbs 18:21 says, "Death and life are in the power of the tongue: and they that love it shall eat the fruit thereof."

Whatever we say will essentially come to pass if we say it in the divine will of the Lord. In John 15:7, Jesus promised, "If ye abide in me, and my words abide in you, ye shall ask what ye will, and it shall be done unto you." If we are connected to the Source of power, we can expect power to flow into our lives. We will be able to walk in victory and not in defeat because of the awesome authority God has given to us as believers.

Elijah the Tishbite expressed this authority when he told King Ahab, "As the LORD God of Israel liveth, before whom I stand, there shall not be dew nor rain these years, but according to my word" (1 Kings 17:1). What gave Elijah the courage and ability to say this? It was the fact that the God of Israel was within him, and he served God on a daily basis. He had come to a place of power and authority to speak words that lived because he was connected to the eternal power Source.

> And this is the confidence that we have in him, that, if we ask any thing according to his will, he heareth us: And if we know that he hear us, whatsoever we ask, we know that we have the petitions that we desired of him.
>
> —1 John 5:14–15

If we are attached to Christ and He dwells in us, we know that we are asking what He has put into our spirit. Therefore, we can be confident that He will grant what we say. Although negative thoughts come to detour our focus from our God-given authority to speak life, we can speak good things, not bad things, in our homes and our life situations. We can speak blessings, not curses, over our marriage and our children. Rather than give strength to darkness by murmuring and complaining, we can give strength to the angels to come to our rescue as we speak good things about God's many benefits to us (Ps. 103).

The Spirit of Hatred and the Spirit of Bitterness

The spirit of negativity is often expressed in hatred, which can be defined as "an intense dislike for something or somebody."

Marc Lépine, a French Canadian man, suffered the terrible consequences of severe hatred. By the age of twenty-five, Lépine had developed a deep hatred for women and also had an obsession with war and violence. In December 1989, Lépine burst into a classroom at the University of Montreal with an automatic gun in his hand and directed the men to one side of the room and the women to the other. Finally he let out some curse words against feminists and opened fire into the crowd of women students, taking fourteen lives that day. Then he turned the gun on himself and took his own life.

Hatred can take the form of prejudice that grows from one person feeling that he is better than another person. (Please read the essay "Prejudice: Just a Zebra" in Appendix C.) It is also closely related to bitterness, which is characterized by an attitude that is "harshly reproachful, marked by cynicism and rancor, intensely unpleasant." No one can ever get things right for a bitter person. Bitterness takes him on a trail of trying to find completeness in someone or something, and it is a futile search. Often, bitterness will paralyze a person for many years because he is always looking at who did what to him. Even when love is shown to a bitter person, he rejects it totally. Offenses he has suffered keep him from feeling or being capable of feeling love.

If a person is bitter, it comes across loud and clear even though he may try to conceal it. A bitter person will always express negative thoughts, even in a message or speech for a pleasant, wonderful occasion. If bitterness is in the heart, it will come through the mouth. An individual who is always sharp or demeaning even when it seems that all is going well has a root of bitterness in his heart.

Bitterness breeds destruction, not only for oneself but for others, too. One person who was extremely bitter blamed others for the things he had suffered, even though he himself had caused most of his pain by poor choices he had made. However, instead of recognizing that he was his own worst enemy, he continually badgered others and caused them to be alienated from him. He died alone without companionship, without family, without a wife, and without children.

Many people die in bitterness because they allow it to grow from hurt, pain, and disappointments. Failure in relationships can cause bitterness of heart if we do not look for an opportunity to try again. A woman had multiple failures in marriage, even to the point that one spouse was abusive to her and sexually abused her child. Another spouse was an alcoholic, and yet she continued to try and wanted to have someone to love her. She became so bitter and disgruntled that she essentially felt she should just die. It seemed that failure was in her, and she thought something must be wrong with her. But right at the moment when she had almost told the Lord, "Just take me out of this world," He blessed her with a wonderful husband who loves and adores her. She is very happy to this day.

Barrenness can cause one to be bitter. A woman who was married to a physician was unable to bear him any children, even though she tried and tried. She became very bitter and drowned her sorrows in alcohol, while her husband was having multiple affairs. One day, however, she decided to turn from the false comfort of alcohol and bathe in the Word of God instead. She found peace.

Job had reasons to be bitter. As Job 1 and 2 tell us, he lost his livestock, his children, and finally his health, all "without cause" (Job 2:3). Although he could have become bitter, Job decided to wait on God and trust in Him. At times his thoughts and feelings toward God were, "Why have you forsaken me, Lord? Why have you done this to me, Lord?" However, he repented of these thoughts and feelings when he truly realized the greatness of God. He forgave his friends who falsely accused him and even prayed for them. As he did, the Lord not only restored his health, but gave him much more than he had to begin with.

The story of Job encourages us never to give up. We must never allow bitterness and disappointment to overtake us and overshadow us. The apostle Paul wrote:

> Let all bitterness, and wrath, and anger, and clamour, and evil speaking, be put away from you, with all malice: And be ye kind one to another, tenderhearted, forgiving one another, even as God for Christ's sake hath forgiven you.
>
> —Ephesians 4:31–32

God has forgiven us, and we also should forgive one another. We must not harbor bitterness, hurt, pain, ill feelings, and anger in our hearts, for they will encourage other spirits, such as murder and violence to come in. Colossians 3:19 reads, "Husbands love your wives and be not bitter against them." Men are to love their wives and not have ill feelings toward them for any reason. If there is any bickering or arguing, we are to quickly dismiss it and cover it with the blood of Christ.

7

VARIANCE, WRATH, STRIFE, SEDITION, AND HERESIES

Now the works of the flesh are manifest, which are these; Adultery, fornication, uncleanness, lasciviousness, Idolatry, witchcraft, hatred, variance, *emulations,* wrath, strife, seditions, heresies.

GALATIANS 5:19–20, EMPHASIS ADDED

ACCORDING TO *WEBSTER'S Dictionary, variance* means "difference; the fact or state of being in disagreement; discord; not in harmony or agreement." Most may be familiar with the mathematical measure of variance, which is the square of the standard deviation. All of these definitions essentially say the same thing—there is a difference that causes a separation or a division.

Differences and division in the spirit world began when Satan tried to exalt himself above God in the heavenlies. After he was cast out of heaven, he used trickery and subtlety to tempt the woman to eat of the tree of knowledge of good and evil. She made a conscious decision to do so, and with that Satan caused a division in her marriage. God had made Adam the head of his house and had instructed him to follow His commandments. Eve made a conscious decision to disobey the Lord and what He had spoken to her husband.

Adam also ate of the forbidden fruit, and both he and Eve were thrown out of the Garden of Eden. They had to leave a paradise so great that they had everything they could possibly want, and they lost the harmony and unity they had enjoyed with God and with each other. It was all destroyed in one moment because of their disobedience. As the last verses of Genesis 3 show, variance, division, separation, and discord now existed between God and mankind and also between Adam and Eve.

Cain and Abel were the first children of Adam and Eve. In the process of time, Cain, a tiller of the ground, brought of the fruit of the ground and offered it unto the Lord. Abel, who was a keeper of sheep, also brought of the firstlings of his flock. Genesis 4:4–5 says that the Lord had respect unto Abel and unto his offering but not unto Cain and his offering. Cain was very upset because of this, and his countenance fell.

God responded to Cain in verses 6–7 and said, "Why are you angry? And why has your countenance fallen? If you do well, will you not be accepted? And if you do not do well, sin lies at the door. And its desire is for you, but you should rule over it" (NKJV).

Here, at the beginning of the human race, we can see the

first actual generational curse. The curse of division and discord that had come upon Adam and Eve passed down to the relationship between Cain and Abel. While Abel was trying all he knew to walk uprightly before the Lord, Cain hated his brother for doing good. Bitterness took root in his heart, and he allowed the spirit of murder to come and grow within him. He killed his brother, and, of course, produced an ungodly line, as seen in Genesis 4:16–24. In God's plan, Adam and Eve bore another son, who took the place of Abel. His name was Seth.

The tragedy of variance, discord, and strife continued in Genesis 27, when Jacob stole Esau's blessing. Esau had already given his birthright to Jacob in exchange for a bowl of stew. Now, Jacob tricked his father by putting animal hair around him and going in to his father to receive the blessing of the inheritance.

Immediately after Isaac had blessed Jacob in verse 22–29, Esau went in to his father to receive the same blessing. In verse 35, Isaac told him, "Thy brother came with subtilty, and hath taken away thy blessing." Esau, of course, was so angry with Jacob that he sought to kill him. He hated Jacob because he had taken that which was rightfully his. Out of division and discord grew bitterness and the spirit of murder. Jacob, however, ran away before his brother could execute his plan.

The Bible has recorded many stories of the continuing problem of variance, and one notable example is the devastating division that happened when Rehoboam became king after the death of his father, King Solomon (1 Kings 12). The people of Israel asked Rehoboam to make their yoke of service less grievous than it had been under his father. In response to this, Rehoboam consulted with the old men, who had stood before Solomon before he died, and also with the young men, who had grown up with him. The old men, who were full of wisdom, advised him to lighten the load of the people, but the young men said to make it harder on them.

Rehoboam chose to follow the counsel of the young men and told the Israelites that he would add to the yoke his father had placed on them. His action caused a split in the kingdom, and ten of the tribes left Rehoboam to form another kingdom under a leader named Jereboam. Only the tribes of Judah and Benjamin remained under the rule of Rehoboam. Tragically, the two kingdoms battled against each other, and much bloodshed resulted from the discord between them.

Wrath, Strife, Sedition, and Heresies

Wrath is a "violent, resentful anger, or rage." Even though wrath is listed as a separate work of the flesh, it can technically be classed with variance. Wrath comes with division, bitterness, and anger. As we have seen in the story of Cain and Abel, wrath will progress to violence and murder if we allow it. Wrath is closely related to strife, which has been defined as "bitter, sometimes violent conflict" or "exertion or contention for superiority."

Webster's Dictionary says that sedition is "conduct or language that incites others to rebel against the authority of the estate; rebellion, insurrection." We witnessed the grievous work of sedition in the division that came to Israel at the beginning of Rehoboam's reign. Satan was cast out of heaven because of his act of sedition, and he continues to bring much discord through it today.

The term *heresies* refers to "an opinion or doctrine in conflict with established religious beliefs, distinction from or denial of the Roman Catholic dogma by a professed believer or baptized church member." One example of the work of heresies is the founding of the Jehovah's Witnesses. According to Dr. Bobby Bean, the Jehovah's Witness religion was started because its founder, Charles Russell of Pittsburgh, Pennsylvania, had a fear of hell. Russell would oftentimes write graffiti on walls and express this fear. Therefore, he made sure that his doctrine did not teach the existence of hell. He rejected much of the Christian theology and practices.[1]

The Impact of Small Differences

When there is variance in a church or denomination, very small differences can bring about the establishment of another church or denomination. In many instances millions of people have experienced great changes because of one particular incident or one particular issue. If we compare the various denominations, we notice that most of them have very small differences that caused one man to go one direction and another man another direction. For example, if we look at the Methodist, Church of God in Christ, and Baptist denominations, we see very slight differences in theological beliefs. However, as Dr. Bean has written, they are enough to cause three separate denominations.

John Wesley (1703–1791), the founder of the Methodist Movement, is considered the spiritual and intellectual father of the Holiness and Pentecostal Movement. The son of an Anglican preacher, he was educated at Oxford University in England, and his studying influenced him to seek after holiness and perfection. The Methodist Holiness Movement took off in the United States after the Civil War and appeared to increase until the mid-1880s. A conflict arose over the issues of the many works of grace and the perfection of God, and, in 1880, Daniel Water organized the Church of God with headquarters in Anderson, Indiana.

The Methodist denomination was threatened by the Holiness Movement and felt that it should stand against it. After the 1880s several independent Holiness churches were established: the Church of God, the Church of God and Holiness, and Holiness Church of California. These churches differed on beliefs about "holy living" and also about the way baptism and the Lord's Supper are to be executed. These were very thin, fine lines, but they provided enough variance to cause the formation of different churches, denominations, and organizations.

The Fire-Baptized Church was organized in 1895. This church believed in dancing, rejoicing, laughing in the Spirit, and was supposedly the first church to teach the baptism of the Holy Ghost. The Church of God in Christ, the largest Pentecostal denomination in the United States, was founded by Bishop Charles Harrison Mason in 1897. Bishop Mason was born September 8, 1866, on Pryor Farm in Memphis, Tennessee, to Jerry and Eliza Mason. They were members of the Missionary Baptist Church, and young Charles Mason enrolled in Arkansas Baptist College in Little Rock, Arkansas, but withdrew after a few months because of its method of teaching and its presentation of the Bible message.

Bishop Mason went to the Azuza Street Revival in Los Angeles, California, in 1907 to hear the of preaching of Elder William Seymour and to experience the outpouring of the Holy Ghost. As the Word of God was preached, he earnestly wanted the baptism of the Holy Ghost. However, he had a choice to go and pray either with those who wanted salvation or with those who wanted to receive the Holy Ghost. Bishop Mason humbled himself and went first to the lower place with those who wanted salvation, even though he felt he was saved. He wanted no obstacles, no pride. Then he went to the second place of prayer, where he received the baptism of the Holy Ghost.

Since the Baptist church did not believe in speaking in tongues nor the fire of the Holy Ghost at that time, Bishop Mason did not continue in it. He said that the Lord spoke to him through 1 Thessalonians 2:14, "For ye, brethren, became followers of the churches of God which in Judaea are in Christ Jesus: for ye also have suffered like things of your own countrymen, even as they have of the Jews." This was how God gave him the name of the denomination we know as the Church of God in Christ. And of course, the Assemblies of God denomination was born from the Church of God in Christ.

The Power of Agreement in Christ

There is power in agreement. Genesis 11:1–4 tells how the people, who all spoke only one language, began to build a tower that they felt would reach to heaven. In verses 5–8, God recognized that they were one in unity and strength and that they would accomplish whatever they set out to do. Therefore, He came down from heaven to confuse their language and scatter them over all the earth.

The Book of Nehemiah confirms the power of agreement in its account of how Nehemiah and the people of Jerusalem were able to complete the task of rebuilding the walls of the city. They did it because there was unity and strength.

However, when two people have two different visions, there is "di-vision." *Di*, means "two," and di-vision happens when the devil creates discord and strife in marriages and between people who should have a common vision. He uses the weapons of faultfinding, blame, bitterness, and unforgiveness to keep them at war with each other. One result of this is that the members of Christ's body will tend to hinder each other instead serving together as instruments in God's kingdom. Worse yet is the awful possibility that we will bite and devour one another and be consumed (Gal. 5:15).

In spite of this, we can be victorious over Satan's purpose to steal, kill, and destroy (John 10:10). We can know the power of unity and the strength that comes by being one with each other in prayer. Jesus described the strength and power we have in marriage, as a church, or as a major corporation when we are unified by agreement in prayer in the following passage:

> Verily I say unto you, Whatsoever ye shall bind on earth shall be bound in heaven: and whatsoever ye shall loose on earth shall be loosed in heaven. Again I say unto you, That if two of you shall agree

> on earth as touching any thing that they shall ask, it shall be done for them of my Father which is in heaven. For where two or three are gathered together in my name, there am I in the midst of them.
>
> —Matthew 18:18–20

Christ promised that He is in the midst of two or more people who join together to agree with each other in prayer to Him for any particular thing that is in His will. He is there. He further said that whatever is bound on earth—the negative things, the things that are not of God—are also bound in heaven. In other words, if the spirit of lack, the spirit of financial need, the spirit of hate, the spirit of lust are bound on earth, they are bound in heaven. Those things that are loosed on earth—peace, joy, and love—are loosed in heaven.

We must learn to know the power and authority we have by agreeing together in Christ Jesus. Through Him we can conquer variance, wrath, strive, seditions, and heresies. We can be victorious in our homes, our churches, and the corporations where we work. As we touch and agree for God's miraculous working in our lives, we can walk in daily victory. Jesus is Lord. He is still on the throne.

8

EMULATIONS, ENVYINGS, AND MURDERS

Now the works of the flesh are manifest, which are these; Adultery, fornication, uncleanness, lasciviousness, Idolatry, witchcraft, hatred, variance, emulations, *wrath, strife, seditions, heresies,* Envyings, murders.

GALATIANS 5:19–21, EMPHASIS ADDED

EMULATION, ACCORDING TO *Webster's Dictionary,* is "ambition or effort to equal or surpass another; imitation of another; jealousy, rivalry." Envy is "resentful desire for another's possession or advantage, covetousness." It means that one wants a particular thing that belongs to someone else, not necessarily another thing like it, to legitimately be his own.

Emulation and envy, jealousy and covetousness are very cruel, heartless, and ruthless. They can cause the conception of murder and destruction if they are allowed to reign in one's heart and mind. The Bible gives many instances of how these evil spirits caused terrible harm in the lives of Cain and Abel and also Jacob and Esau. However, in my opinion, the epitome of emulation and envying is seen in the story of Joseph and his brothers in Genesis 30 through 50.

Joseph was the son of Jacob, born to Rachel in Jacob's older years. Although Jacob had six sons before Joseph, he gave Joseph, who was his favorite son, a coat of many colors (Gen. 37:3). When Joseph's brothers saw that their father loved Joseph more than all of them, they hated Joseph and did not speak in a friendly way to him.

When Joseph began to dream, his brothers hated him more. In Genesis 37:7 Joseph described his dream and said, "For, behold, we were binding sheaves in the field, and, lo, my sheaf arose, and also stood upright; and, behold, your sheaves stood round about, and made obeisance to my sheaf." To this, his brothers replied, "Surely we will not bow down to you." Then Joseph had another dream in which he saw the sun and the moon, meaning his father and mother, and the eleven stars, his brothers, bow down to him. Genesis 37:11 says that his brothers envied him, and his father took notice of what he had said.

In their envy and jealousy, Joseph's brothers decided that they had to get rid of him. And even though they denied that what he said was truth, they knew in their hearts that he would end up being the head of them. Therefore, when Joseph came to see them at Jacob's command as they were feeding their father's flock in Shechem, they took him and cast him into a pit. Although Joseph didn't know it at the time, it was necessary for him to be thrown into the pit so he could be elevated to the place the Lord had for him.

As Joseph's brothers were eating, they say a company of Ishmaelites traveling to Egypt and sold Joseph to them. After killing a young goat and dipping Joseph's coat in the blood, they brought the coat to their father and told him that they had found it that way. A heartbroken Jacob mourned the loss of his son, with the belief that Joseph had been torn to pieces by a wild animal.

When Joseph arrived in Egypt, Potiphar, an officer of Pharaoh, bought him to be a slave in his house. Even though Joseph was a slave, Potiphar saw the potential in him and elevated him to the overseer in his house. Potiphar's wife saw that Joseph was a handsome young man, and she sought to have a physical relationship with him. However, Joseph denied her and even ran from her. He told her, "Your husband has given me responsibility for everything in the house except you, because you are his wife." A reason of greater importance, Joseph declared, was that he did not want to sin against God Almighty.

Because Joseph refused to have a relationship with Potiphar's wife, she accused him of making sexual advances toward her. Potiphar accepted the word of his wife and put Joseph into the Egyptian prison. While he was there, however, the Lord again elevated him to a place of authority. In addition, he met the king's butler and the king's baker, who had also been put into prison. One morning, they told Joseph they had each had a dream the night before. God gave Joseph the interpretation of both dreams, and he told the butler that he would be released from prison in three days and restored to his place in the palace. He would once again deliver Pharaoh's cup to him. The interpretation of the baker's dream was not so good. In three days, he would lose his life by hanging on a tree.

When Joseph told the king's butler that he would be restored to his position in the palace, he asked the butler to remember him when it happened. For some time, however, the butler did not remember Joseph. But when Pharaoh had a dream and was troubled by it, the butler remembered Joseph. He told Pharaoh about Joseph, and the ruler sent for Joseph, who interpreted Pharaoh's dream. Joseph told Pharaoh that there would be seven years of plenty followed by seven years of famine. He advised Pharaoh to look for someone wise to be in charge of gathering food in the good years so that there would be provisions in the time of famine. Pharaoh appointed Joseph as that person.

And so, Joseph went from the pit to the palace. It was a divine plan of the Lord to use the jealousy that was in his brothers' hearts to get into the palace. When Joseph met his brothers again, they were seeking food because they were hungry. Instead of retaliating and doing evil to them, Joseph fed them. He brought not only them but also his father and all his kinsmen to a land of plenty; he blessed them. Instead of returning evil for evil against his brothers, he gave them good. He loved them as his brothers and as his kinsmen.

Rivalry That Destroys Relationships

Emulation and envying can be expressed in rivalry that occurs when friends or coworkers desire the same position or sometimes the same husband or wife. We do not expect this to happen because friendship between two people is a relationship of value and trust that has been established by the investment of time and effort. Regretfully, however, betrayal can destroy close relationships.

For example, the president of a company may set out to help all who are in the company, especially those who have been faithful. The intent of his heart is to help promote people who have been forgotten, especially friends who are very capable in their knowledge and abilities. In this setting, his friend may desire to be president instead of him because she wants the power and authority. She may be able to win his position through popularity even though she does not really care about the company or have the training and experience it requires.

Or a man may like his best friend's wife as well, and he may successfully win her away. This has happened over and over again, sometimes when children are involved and other times when they are not. Or perhaps a woman has a husband who is very kind to her. She tells a friend about him, and the friend decides that she wants him to be that good to her instead. The friend seduces the husband and marries him. Sadly, this too has happened.

The negative results of such rivalry are manifold: high blood pressure, stroke, nervous conditions, ulcers, diabetes, heart attacks, cancer, and death. Depression, loss of interest in life, and loss of sleep are some other consequences of emulation and envying, as well as jealousy and covetousness.

The Contrast Between Jealousy and God's Purpose

Severe jealousy results in great tragedy that may include murders, the work of the flesh that follows envyings in Galatians 5:21. In one instance, a minister and his wife decided to split up because of their differences. The wife married another man, who eventually ended up in jail. And after a time, the minister rededicated his life to the Lord. He was convinced that he could win back the love and devotion of his ex-wife, even though she was married again. As time progressed, the minister was not able to win his ex-wife back. He felt that if he could not have her, he did not want anyone to have her. He got a gun and killed his ex-wife and then himself. His jealousy and covetousness caused his spirit to be open, and a spirit of murder eventually came into him when he could not get the one thing he wanted more than anything else.

Yet, God is able to deliver us from jealousy if we listen to His voice and obey Him. One Christian woman visited a local church, where a very nice lady was asked to give the alter call and pray for those who came forward. When the invitation was given for people with special needs, the visiting woman mocked the prayer minister. She refused to come and receive prayer even though the prayer minister specifically asked her to do so. She was truly jealous of how the Lord was using the prayer minister and felt that she had no right to pray for her.

The prayer minister told the visiting woman that she would

be glad to receive prayer after the next week because of what was about to happen to her. The next week the visiting woman was diagnosed with breast cancer. She had surgery and went through many trials and tribulations for one year. After therapy she still remained very ill. It appeared that there was no hope until the woman with cancer yielded herself to the voice of the Lord. "Go to the prayer minister and repent for disrespecting the anointing of the Holy Spirit that she walked in," God told her, "and ask her to pray for you." The woman who had cancer did what the Lord instructed her to do and was immediately and totally healed. She has had no more problems with the cancer since her healing ten years ago.

Emulations and envying are expressed in the struggle for power and success. Sadly, serious problems can result from this struggle, depending on how one measures success. I believe that success is finding the purpose of God and walking in His purpose. Whether we are at the top of the line or at the bottom, we must find our purpose in God and walk in it.

This is what Pete Maravich did after God softened his crusty heart. On a radio show hosted by Dr. James Dobson, Maravich told how he at first refused God when He called him to be a Christian. He went on to play professional basketball, had his own jet, had been to see the president, had a mansion, had everything a person could ever want in life. Yet, he was not happy. Then God called him again, and this time he answered in the affirmative. He found God's purpose for his life, and from that point on, he said, he had never been happier.

Maravich played ball for many years. One day, while he was doing physical exercises, it was discovered that he had a congenital heart disease. He had placed his body under much physical stress, which could have caused his death. However, the Lord, by His mercy and grace, allowed Maravich to turn and give his life to Him before he died. And when God took him home as he was sleeping, he finally found what success truly is.[1]

9

OFFENSES

It is a beautiful, sunny day. You awake with the determination to start a new exercise program that will help you get into shape over the next year. As you share your heart with those close to you, your best friend comments, "You've never lost any weight. You never have and you never will. You might as well eat and just forget that silly exercise program." Immediately a feeling of defeat comes over you. "Maybe I can't," you think. You have a sense of despair as you realize that your best friend does not believe in your ability to follow through on the thing you so desperately want to do.

This is only one of the many ways we may suffer an offense. What is an offense? An offense is "the act of causing anger, displeasure, and resentment." An offense brings insult. It causes one to stumble and presents an occasion to sin. It slows down progression in our lives and interferes with the goal or destiny set before us. An offense does not just occur, but it is originated or manipulated by something or someone. As long as we live in the world, we will face hurtful words and actions that offend us spiritually, mentally, and physically. In these experiences, we may find that we have a total loss of focus and vision and purpose. We may find it very difficult to get over an offense.

This, however, is not what God desires for us. When someone makes a negative comment such as, "That doesn't look good," we must realize that everyone's taste is different.

Many people believe that if they stay to themselves, read their Bible, and go to church, they will be untouchable, secure from the world and its cruel intentions and offenses. The truth, however, is quite to the contrary. In Matthew 18:7 Jesus said, "Woe unto the world because of offences! for it must needs be that offences come; but woe to that man by whom the offence cometh!" When we consider this, we must ask ourselves, What are the consequences of this statement or action? What will result from it in my life personally and also in the lives of others?

Failure, Guilt, Disrespect, Lies

In the illustration that opened this chapter, we saw how one's expectation that another person will fail can be a source of offense. This highlights the fact that failure is an offense that can cause us to become very discouraged. We must learn to look at failures as trials and not allow them to stop the progression of our work. We must take the approach of Benjamin Franklin and Thomas Edison, who had hundreds of trials before attaining success. In fact, Edison once said, "Genius? Nothing! Sticking to it is the genius…I've failed my way to success."[1] We should take a close look at the results we are trying to achieve. If we have tried the same thing twenty times and received the same results, perhaps it is time to consider an alternate method.

The children of Israel experienced failure as they wandered in the wilderness for forty years. This did not happen because the Lord wanted it to, but because their behavior continued in the cycle of unbelief that long until they finally got it right. A trip that should have taken about a week took forty years because they refused to learn the lesson of trusting God and following his leadership. They needed to believe God for all things because He had proven Himself by giving them water in dry places and feeding them quail at their request.

Guilt is an offense that may result from failure of any type. It brings us into an "it's my fault syndrome" that says, "If it had not been for me, it would never have happened." For example, children of divorced couples often feel that they are responsible for the death of their parents' marriage. Some children express their belief that if their behavior had been better or their mom or dad would not have had to fuss at them so much, their parents would still be together. Other children think that they asked for too many things and thereby caused their parents to argue, fight, and finally divorce. What tremendous pressure for a child to carry! Many children don't express their feelings of guilt to their parents or to anyone, but they are tormented by this offense for years. Some go into adulthood and marriage without facing it. If the parent who has caused the guilt in a child's life gives the reassurance that the child is not at fault for what happened, it helps tremendously and puts the child at ease. It may not take away all the anxiety, but it does help to alleviate the guilt.

Two very insulting offenses are disrespect and lies. Disrespect steals the honor that is due a person. It can be quiet and subtle or loud and boisterous. However, it can cause great emotional trauma to people who are not sure about who they are. A lie can cause much damage to one's character, and it can be almost debilitating even when one knows the truth. However, if a person knows who he or she is, time has a way of allowing truth to come forth. Some react to disrespect by showing the strength of their authority and starting a cycle of vengeance. To suffer the offences of disrespect and lies can lead to a stressful life unless one is able to find peace.

Rejection

The spirit of rejection is another offense that has deeply wounded many people. Rejection is the feeling that one has little or no worth even if he has achieved greatness in life. Usually rejection will cause a person to say, "Look what I am doing. Is it good enough to satisfy you? Does this make you proud of me yet?" To feel rejected is to feel like one has been overlooked or, even worse, discarded. If rejection is allowed to continue in adults or children, it lends itself to bitterness, violence, and physical ailments.

One tragic example of the destructive result of rejection is seen in the life of Charles Manson, who never formed a relationship with his mother. After his first murder, a serial killing streak began. But who was he really trying to kill?

Perhaps he was trying to hurt his mother for neglecting and rejecting him.[2]

However, the offense of rejection can be overcome with the spirit of forgiveness. We see this in the story of a woman who was rejected by her mother and stepfather when she was a young girl in Germany. She was very bitter and, at age thirteen, came to the United States, where she eventually got a job at a hospital in New York City. She was married and had a daughter, but her husband left her after having multiple affairs. She was always bitter and hurt over everything that people did, and her life was filled with complaints. Though her heart was very kind and she would gladly give her last cent to anyone, she continually talked about others taking advantage of her.

Because of the bitterness this woman expressed in her home, her daughter wanted to leave as soon as she was able. The daughter found joy in attending church, but one Sunday while her mother was enjoying the service, the daughter was raped by one of the pastors. The daughter didn't tell her mother or anyone for almost thirty years but became very bitter and angry. She did not attend church or acknowledge Jesus as Lord for almost thirty years after the incident because she felt that God had forsaken her. She also started to hate her mother because she blamed her for the rape, partially because she felt she had pushed her father out of her life.

The mother sank into the lowest state of bitterness and depression and pushed all who attempted to help her away, even though she attended church and said she was a Christian. Further, she developed cancer and felt that nothing good would ever happen in her life. Yet, through her pain and suffering a great revelation miraculously came to her. One day she realized that out of all the children her mother had, she was never raped, hurt, or harmed physically. In fact, the favor of the Lord had come to her in a greater way than it had to any of her sisters and brothers.

At that moment she let go of the past and a tender side that had never been seen in her before emerged. Many scriptures had been quoted to her before, but that day she believed the scripture and deliverance came. Due to the release of her bitterness and her forgiveness toward others, the cancer did not progress. Though she had been given only months to live, she lived ten more years.

The daughter followed in her mother's initial footsteps of bitterness for years because that was all she knew. She married a man who had four children by different women and broke her mother's heart. Her husband loved her but he also loved many other women and made it clear that their marriage did not detour his relationships with his other lovers. He even had a relationship with his daughter, while she was at work. She tried to be bitter with everyone she met. She had married to get away from home because she was tired of her mother but her worst nightmare came true; she became her mother.

Unlike her mother, she abused her children by beating them unmercifully and verbally abusing them. She began to overeat to try to ease her pain but nothing would help. Her oldest son became involved with gangs. He was angry at the world and especially bitter with his mother. The other son, who was seemingly quiet, had violent outbursts. Her three daughters became very sexually promiscuous.

The daughter decided to commit suicide and end all her pain, but first she was determined to make a very joyful coworker mad. She tried and tried, but no matter how badly she treated her coworker, the lady continued to show love and kindness to her. Finally, after weeks of failing in her attempts to change the character of the lady, she asked why she was so nice. The lady responded by pointing her to Christ and His power. As a result, she received Christ, and for the first time, confessed the rape and the hatred she had for the church.

The bitterness resolved when she forgave her mother, the minister who raped her, and the husband who was repeatedly unfaithful to her. Her children also gave their lives to the Lord. Her son left the gang and began ministering for the Lord. He forgave his mother for her offenses against him because Jesus forgave him for all his sin. Her other children also began to seek a relationship with the Lord. She began again with her mother to establish not only love but also a friendship they had never had before. Now they could truly love one another through the eyes of Christ.

The Death of a Loved One

One of the offenses we suffer, perhaps many times, is the loss of a loved one in death. This is true whether the death is timely or untimely and whether the person is old or young. Some people become angry with God for taking a very gracious, kind loved one and feel that it is totally unfair. They wonder why He couldn't take some mean or nasty person instead. A mother who carries her baby to term only to see it born dead may struggle with the question, Why my child? Especially if she has not had any other children, she may become bitter toward mothers who have healthy children.

Sometimes people will deny being angry but still grieve for years. They may become disheartened and withdrawn and even lose hope for living. Some husbands or wives tend not to want to make love with each other because they are grieving, while others do it as an outlet for their grief. The actions of grief can take us into a destructive, depressive state if we allow it to, but we do not have to let this happen. Instead, we can accept it as a bitterness that will lessen in time. Although it is natural to grieve for a season, we must daily let go of the hurt and pain we suffer from the loss of our loved ones. We must believe that God is like a gardener who knows when a flower is ready to be picked to give the sweetest fragrance.

The following story shows God knows how to help us when we lose a loved one. A woman had a beautiful daughter who was so gifted and talented that many colleges readily accepted her. The young lady, who loved the Lord with everything that was in her, died before her second year of college. The mother, a Christian, had another daughter and a son left, but she was very angry with God and could not let her grief go. It was in this state that she developed breast cancer and was told she would live only six months or less. As she turned to God, He said, "I only had one son, and I gave him up. But I have left you with two children." She repented and has lived about forty years since then.

A Lesson from the Life of Peter

We who are in the body of Christ have various experiences that may cause offense. This is very clearly seen in the life of the apostle Peter, a fisherman who was called to be a disciple of Christ. Peter received a revelation that could come only from God when he proclaimed that Jesus was the Christ, the Son of the living God (Matt. 16:16). He witnessed the transfiguration of Christ, recorded in Matthew 17:1–9.

Peter saw many miracles and even was a part of some of them. He walked on the water when Jesus told Him to come to him on the Sea of Galilee. When he took his eyes off Jesus and began to sink, the Lord reached out and rescued him (Matt. 14:28–31). Before walking on the water, he had seen Jesus feed a multitude of five thousand men, plus women and children, with five loaves and two fish—and still have leftovers (Matt. 14:13–21).

The night before Jesus died, He told Peter that he would deny Him three times before the rooster crowed (Matt. 26:33–35). Although Peter was convinced he would never do this, he was afraid for his life after Jesus was arrested. He forgot all the miracles he had seen and experienced, and he did deny the Lord and even cursed for emphasis the third time (Matt. 26:73–74). Although he wept bitterly about this and appeared repentant, the condemnation was greater than he could tolerate. He had let the Lord down, and he, along with some of his brothers in Christ, went back to fishing.

He had not been delivered from many things. He cursed, after he denied Christ at the crucifixion of Jesus (Matt. 26:74).

He had a terrible temper and even cut off the ear of a soldier who was trying to arrest Jesus (John 18:10–11). Jesus admonished him to put away his sword because if he lived by it, then he faced the consequence of perishing or being destroyed by the same thing (Matt. 26:51–52).

Jesus loved Peter in spite of all that he had done, and He personally restored him after the Resurrection. Three times, He asked Peter if he loved Him and instructed him to feed His sheep. Although Peter felt unworthy because of his past, the Lord saw his future. The Lord saw what Peter was going to become, not where he was spiritually at that moment (John 21:1–19).

Some give up when they fail the Lord and say, "I just can't do this." However, we must never give up. If we make a mistake, we have an advocate with the Father. When we ask the Lord to forgive us, He forgives us and restores us. Peter became so anointed by God's power, many were healed when his shadow passed over them (Acts 5:15).

We cannot look at man or to man for validation because we may be offended. Instead, we must look to the One who, though He was tempted, knew no sin.

10

ABUSE

ABUSE IS A very common offense that happens daily in the lives of many in our world. Because of the negative impact of this very destructive tool, it is important that we be aware of the forms it may take. In this chapter, we will discuss mental abuse (my focus will be on child neglect), verbal abuse, physical abuse, and sexual abuse.

Mental Abuse

Mental abuse can be a source of offense to people of any age, However, it is important to recognize that a person is most vulnerable to the effects of offenses at birth. As a child's life begins, many agents shape the development of its spiritual, mental, and physical growth. God's ideal is that a child be born into an environment in which it has been eagerly expected. In that kind of environment, the mother begins to bond with the child, usually within hours of delivery, and the child becomes dependent on its parents for protection, nurturing, and love.

However, many children do not bond with their parents or guardians. Thus, they continually seek the love and approval of others to fill this void. When they are repeatedly denied bonding, affection, and love, they tend to seek other forms of acceptance, which usually ends with destruction, pain, and hardships. Children who experience this lack of caring suffer neglect, a type of mental abuse.

Neglected children continually seek affirmation and a sense of self-worth. When they fail to fill this void through healthy relationships with their parents or guardians, they begin to express their pain first with actions as simple as misbehaving. The intensity of their actions may increase to biting, hitting, or fighting others; throwing temper tantrums; or setting fires. These behaviors may escalate to robberies and sometimes murder if the offense is not released. Some children end up in gangs because they want to belong to a group that seems to care. They are looking for acceptance, security, and love.

This response to neglect is not true only of children of the poor, but it is also very common among those who are affluent, financially and socially elite. It occurs with any parents or guardians who don't spend quality time with their children or are not aware of what is happening in their lives. There are, of course, exceptions to any situation. Sometimes children join gangs and get involved with crime even though their parents have played an active and crucial part of their lives.

Neglect also finds it way into the hearts of adoptive children. They wonder, "Why would my parents give me away? What was so wrong with me, what was so bad about me that I had to be given away? What did I do wrong?" They see adoption as a punishment, and they usually seek to find their natural mother and or father even if they grow up in loving homes. Some tend to have what we call a chip on their shoulders. They may feel that everyone is against them, and they may try to appear humble when they really have an air of superiority.

A number of adoptive children have low self-esteem. Some of them are convinced that they are always right and are plagued by some type of addiction, which they run to whenever they feel defeated. Those addictions can be sex, drugs, or food. A vicious cycle occurs with those addictions as an insult leads to an offense and then addiction. The cycle continues to unfold in shame, guilt, depression, and a greater depth of addiction. It gets worse and worse unless the offense is released.

Anything that disturbs a child's peace of mind can be classified as mental abuse. Sweetly telling them in a nurturing and quiet fashion that they will never amount to anything is still abuse. So is telling them that green monsters are coming to get them or making them stay up all night as a punishment. Children who suffer mental abuse usually end up with tormenting fears. Unless deliverance occurs, they have a hard time functioning in marriage and usually resent their parents when they are adults. Some children who were abused tend to follow the same abusive behavior they suffered unless the offense is released.

In one example of mental abuse, a little boy was forced to witness his father having adulterous relationships. After each act, the father threatened to kill the boy if he said anything to his mother. As a result, the child grew up with tormenting fears and eventually began to abuse little boys. This led to depression and thoughts of suicide. He was finally delivered from the mental anguish and abuse when he totally forgave all that had happened to him.

Verbal Abuse

Verbal abuse can occur in the home in a number of ways. It may happen when one parent is abusive to the other parent or when they are mutually abusive to each other. In either case, this can be very destructive to a child's emotional well-being. Children who witness this behavior usually follow the example that has been set before them at home because they tend to feel that it is all right to dishonor their spouse. For example, if a husband verbally abuses his wife in front of his sons, calling her names that belittle and dishonor her as a woman, both the sons and daughters in the home will feel that this is the way a woman should be treated. They, consequently, end up with dysfunctional homes.

Verbal abuse may also be committed by parents against their children. When children are abused, they feel that they have no other choice but to take what is done to them. Usually they feel that they deserve what they get or it would not be so. Abused children tend to abuse other children, and this usually becomes a vicious cycle that continues into adulthood if there is no true deliverance from the offense they have suffered. Verbally abusing a child makes him or her feel that is the only way to communicate.

Children who suffer verbal abuse will tend to have low self-esteem. Some may be loud and others very quiet, but they are all trying to prove to the world that they are all right. Even though some of them are quiet, they tend to have periods of explosive outbursts. They tend to belittle anyone who gets in their way because they feel so bad. The unfortunate thing about verbally abused children is that they tend to marry those who abuse them because it seems natural to them. This trend tends to continue unless the offense is released.

Verbal abuse is very common. It is done without thought, but then the damage is done. A person can respond to the hurt and insult by grieving, getting even, or letting it go. Either of the first two responses will only result in more pain to the people involved and others beyond them. However, if one is able to let go of the hurt, it tends to clear the air and allow for healing of the relationship.

Physical Abuse

Physical abuse occurs in every social and socioeconomic environment, including the church. It may be played out in a number of ways, including through a husband who is abusive to his wife, a wife who is abusive to her husband, and parents who are abusive to their children. In each case, the offense that results in physical abuse will continue unless it is released to God.

Husbands from abusive backgrounds tend to be happy to beat and abuse their wives because, as they say, their wives deserve it. Most of the women who have grown up with physical abuse agree with that lie and say, "I guess I asked for that whipping. He really does love me or he would not whip me." The husband who is abusive to his wife usually has very low self-esteem and takes his frustration out on his wife, even though he insists that he loves her. The woman feels alone, ashamed, and totally disconnected. Yet, most of the time she does not want to tell others about the abuse, and she endures.

Physical abuse is not only committed by the male species against women, but wives may also be abusive to their husbands. I have dealt with a vast number of cases where the wife has abused her husband. Oftentimes, she was abused as a child and was not able to let go of her anger. She feels that she is never good enough and needs constant affirmation from her husband and everyone around her. It is very difficult for her husband to communicate effectively to her because her mind has been programmed so that she cannot receive the good he sincerely intends for her. Her mind always says that his motive is less than innocent. It tells her, "He doesn't really care for me or anything I have."

Abusers, whether they are male or female, always feel that they are the victim and are being mistreated. This has caused many to be unfaithful to their spouse or to just give up on their marriage and leave their spouse. Yet others have fought physically and both have ended up with injuries. Sometimes, death has occurred.

Physical abuse directed against children often manifests in unexplained accidents, burns, or broken limbs. Many times, parents feel remorse after abusing their children, and children who have been abused will protect their parents and cling to them. The abused children feel that their parents truly love them. Children who suffer physical abuse will tend to beat their children when they become parents. They will justify their actions by telling their children that they love them.

They feel that it is all right since it happened to them when they were children. Some parents hate themselves because they abuse their children, but they are so embarrassed by it that they do not seek help.

Some young mothers have a tendency to abuse their children even if they are not from abusive homes. For some girls, motherhood starts very early. These young girls are restricted because they have the responsibility of caring for a child, and this causes bitterness, anger, and resentment to grow in their hearts. They may take out their anger by abandoning their children or abusing them to the point of broken bones, skull fractures, or even death.

Sexual Abuse

Sexual abuse of children causes them to become promiscuous teenagers and adults who have low self-esteem, bitterness, resentment, and anger. Children who are sexually abused feel that this is the way love is shown and that they must allow the offending person to have sex with them. Otherwise, they will be rejected. Of course, the adult makes sure that the child knows this and uses severe threats to keep the child from telling anyone. In some instances, children will not tell anyone, not even their parents, for many years. Sometimes they hold it in until adulthood or death.

Children who are sexually abused grow up feeling they don't have a right to say no to anyone who wants to have sex with them, male or female. These individuals are usually never satisfied with one mate or, in some cases, only heterosexual relationships. They tend to move from relationship to relationship, longing for satisfaction but never finding it in sex. They tend to go deeper and deeper into lascivious acts until they are exhausted and hit bottom.

These people go through life looking for love and emotional bonding that cannot be obtained from a physical relationship. Because their trust was violated by an adult, they lack proper love for themselves and are seeking the kind of love that can only be found in an intimate relationship. As is true of other forms of abuse, those who have been sexually abused will tend to abuse others. Some of them go on to commit rape, not as an act of lust but as an act of violence and bitterness. All these tragic consequences are possible if the offense is not released.

And yet, God is faithful to grant deliverance to all who come to Him with an open spirit to receive. After the mother of a seven-year-old girl died, the father began molesting her and her younger sister. He sexually abused them for over ten years and threatened to kill himself if they did not cooperate with him. He even insisted that they help pay the bills of the house by engaging in prostitution. The two girls, of course, were very scared and reacted to their fear by becoming promiscuous early in life and by drinking and using cocaine at early ages.

The oldest daughter never felt that she was good enough for anything or anyone, and therefore took every criticism as a personal attack on her. She hated her father with every fiber of her being and saw every man as her father disrespecting her, violating her, and not appreciating her efforts. If anyone she was dating even attempted to disagree with her, a fighting spirit would come upon her and she would beat the man without mercy until her violent temper was satisfied.

After this daughter became pregnant out of wedlock, she got married. Her marriage failed, but one day she decided to give Jesus a try. On a Wednesday night, she was instantly delivered from crack, cocaine, and alcohol by the Word of God, without any type of structured program. Although it took years, by hearing and applying the Word of God, she was also delivered from her low self-esteem, saying yes to those who approached her for sex, and the fighting spirit. She remarried and was very happy.

11

STRESS

WHEN AN OFFENSE, whether it be a spoken word or an abusive action, is rehearsed over and over in the mind, it turns disappointments and hurt into a form of stress that is very destructive. It is true, as Dr. Slaby's account says, that stress can be good. In the time of cave men, the body's reaction to the introduction of a stressor—an increase in blood pressure and heart rate and dilation of the eyes—was necessary for survival.[1] However, persistent stress is not good because it can cause high cholesterol, high blood pressure, strokes, heart attacks, ulcers, cancer, a decrease in ability to fight infections, and many other diseases. (Please read Appendix A, "A Supplement on Stress," for additional information on stress and the physical effect it has on us.)

Stress can also lead to other problems we may not immediately relate to it. These problems may include low self-esteem, social withdrawal, boredom, poor judgment, suicide attempts, anger, argumentative behavior, missing work or school, and alcohol-related car accidents that result in fatalities. Stress may cause drug abuse, smoking, harmful eating patterns (please read Appendix B, "Anorexia Nervosa, Bulimia, and Overeating," for specific examples), tension headaches, teeth grinding, dietary problems, sexual dysfunction, pain without a physical cause, and many more difficulties. Social isolation can lead to depression, which affects relationships at work and also at home with wives, with parents, and possibly with children.

Does God care about our struggles with stress? Yes, He does. One man had migraine headaches for about twelve years and was medically discharged from military service because of his condition. He had been on all types of medication, but when he came into my office, the Lord directed me to tell him to say yes to Him. It was such a simple word, but yes, he dared to say it. Miraculously, he has not had a headache since that time over ten years ago.

In addition to ministering in supernatural ways, God also gives us common-sense ways reduce stress: 1) organize everything you can to decrease chaotic situations; 2) use crisis situations as experiences through which you can learn and benefit; and 3) create an environment that reduces stress. Decorate with colors that are cheerful and bright. Take control of your environment and the life that is set before you. Do not stop living because another person will not participate with you, but identify your goal and make the steps to determine what actions you can do to achieve it.

Life will always include things like death, illness, financial ruin, or success. We cannot change the fact that stressful situations happen, but we must deal with them as they come. While we may have to allow some time to gather resources, we must not procrastinate or put off the things we have to do. That will only add stress to our lives. We must learn to forget the past and let it go. And we must choose friends who will support us. George Elliott said, "The strongest principle of growth lies in human choice."[2]

It is important that we recognize the early signs of stress and get relief. We must reduce xanthine intake in caffeinated substances such as coffee, tea, colas, and eliminate sources of this chemical like cocaine and amphetamines. Xanthine increases one's heart rate, blood pressure, and the oxygen demand on the heart. Caffeine can lead to anxiety and panic, insomnia (not being able to sleep), palpitations (irregular heartbeat), and tachycardia (rapid heart rate).

We must always try to avoid vitamin depletion and maintain optimal levels of vitamins for our nerves and endocrine (glandular) systems to function, especially in stressful times. Particularly important are vitamin C, thiamine (vitamin B1), riboflavin (vitamin B2), niacin, pantothenic acid (vitamin B5), pyridoxine (vitamin B6), and choline. Absence of these vitamins can be associated with cardiovascular, neurological, and sometimes psychiatric problems, which reduce our ability to deal with stress. The symptoms of vitamin depletion can include depression, anxiety, muscle weakness, gastric or stomach upset, and insomnia.

Our salt intake is important, and we must monitor it. Too little salt can lead to weakness, but increased salt leads to fluid or water retention.

Hypoglycemia, which is decreased blood sugar, causes all the body systems to work harder, and we can avoid it by eating small amounts of food every few hours. A person who is not well should use appropriate medication as needed.

We must learn to relax the body and the body muscles. Exercise is very important to increase the strength of the cardiovascular (heart) system, our lungs, and our muscles. Walking and jogging are not only good exercises, but they also allow time to think and possibly explore options of stressful situations. And it is important to get plenty of rest or as much as possible.

Many Christians don't feel that it is possible for stressful situations to drive them to do things such as drinking alcohol or taking drugs. However, even David, in a moment of stress, went to the camp of the enemies, the Philistines, and actively joined with them in 1 Samuel 27. He became one with them and was even willing to fight as one of them because he felt that he had no other place to go. The Lord had to create an environment in which he realized that he could no longer stay with his enemies (1 Sam. 29).

In our response to stress, we must learn to develop a plan and carry it out. (Please read the essays "Peer Pressure: Rock or Clay?" and "Negativity and Stress: Sweating the Small Stuff" in Appendix C.) It is important that we be aware of our strengths and weaknesses and that we guard against our weaknesses being elevated. We must delegate our work and learn how to be selective and not say yes to everything.

Being able to release anger appropriately and channel it the proper way is vital, and we are to treat people the way we want to be treated. Let us guard against saying anything about another if we would not want it said about us. Words hurt, and long after people are gone, the words about them still remain. God's answer to stress is that we build a lifelong spiritual relationship with the one and only living God.

A Painful but Necessary Response

As I mentioned at the beginning of this chapter, destructive forms of stress grow out of offenses that come into our lives. This can happen even when we have not been the direct recipient of an insult. If we choose to transfer the past hurts and pains of others to our present life and then hold on to them, we make ourselves vulnerable to stress.

Many allow partial release of an offense, but that is like putting a Band-Aid on a nick in a major artery. The Band-Aid may slow down the blood loss, but it is not strong enough to stop it so healing and repair can take place. If the loss of blood continues, it will result in death. Since death is not only a physical state but also mental and spiritual, it is possible to have the appearance of functioning normally but not be in touch with the people around us or even be aware of the surroundings. This is the result of a longing and deficit that cannot be filled by anything or anyone on Earth but by God alone.

Another example of how we hold onto offenses is to sweep dirt under a rug. Sooner or later the rug will begin to bulge where the dirt is and eventually someone will trip over that area. Life is like that; we can't ignore, pacify, or sweep offenses to the side. We must address them or they will come back to haunt us when we least expect it. We must thoroughly examine the underlying cause—the root—of the bitterness, hatred, and fear. We must ask ourselves, Why this is happening? Why is it alive and thriving? Is it the result of something that should have died in me a long time ago? This is painful to do, but we must do it with clarity and precision.

The practice of addressing our offenses is vital to receiving healing from stress-related suffering. For example, a woman who had metastasis breast cancer was also filled with unforgiveness and bitterness because of various hurts from other church members and from a long history of family disputes. However, after the diagnosis of her cancer, she was willing to let go of a thirty-year battle with another church member. After praying to this effect, she returned for a second set of X-rays. When the surgeon took new films, he was surprised to find that there was not a trace of cancer.

It is wonderful how the mechanism of the body responds to the emotional state of a person. One young lady suffered with hypertension and had a cancerous lesion that had been documented in three separate office visits in two states. She had multiple stress factors, including children she was extremely concerned about and a husband who was unfaithful. Although she struggled with forgiving her husband and his mistress, she decided to mentally let go of all her past disappointments when she understood that her life was at stake. When the surgeon took a second X-ray, he found that the mass was completely gone. He said somebody must have prayed because the first films had shown cancer, and now it was gone.

A man with severe arthritis in his neck suffered so much

pain that it brought tears to his eyes, and medication was unable to provide any relief. He had come from an abusive background and had left home at an early age to get away from it. However, he had imitated what he had grown up with and was very stern in all his ways. His children hated him, because he did not communicate anything but commands. His wife felt that she was in the way because he made all the decisions without discussing them with her. Finally, he got tired of hurting his wife and children and decided to change his thinking. As he began to let go of his childhood, the pain in his neck was relieved, and his family situation immediately turned around. He began to communicate with his wife and his children and spend time with them. He became an inspiration to many other families that knew how he had changed.

The man's children had begun acting out the results of his abusive behavior. His daughters had started to be promiscuous with men, while his sons had begun smoking and drinking without his knowledge. However, the children began to change as their father reached out to them with love and kindness—a hugging embrace, a tangible expression of care. It was so simple but, oh, so empowering to the family God had given him.

There are thousands upon thousands of cases in which a feeling of offense and disease are related. In some cases, even hearing loss reflects the fact that a person may not want to hear or receive instructions from the Lord. A woman who had been very nice to several ladies in her church congregation discovered that they not only were having an affair with her husband but also were taking things from her house. She reacted to this with an unforgiving heart and became crippled mentally and physically to the point that she could no longer walk. Her fingers became marked with severe arthritis, and finally she could not even get out of bed.

It took about five years to convince her to let go of the past and forgive the women who had offended her so deeply. After that, she began to walk again and have some resolution of the arthritis. However, when she almost died in her late eighties, she was revived and reported an experience of being on a train. She said she could find no peace anywhere she went, nor could she find a place to stop because every area was filled with darkness. It was then that she decided to let go completely of the offenses she had suffered. She lived a few more months before she died in peace.

Relief from Stress

Stress, along with worry and anxiety, brings confusion to the mind. This is a direct attack against God's promise that He would keep him in perfect peace whose mind is stayed on Him because we trust in Him (Isa. 26:3). When we think about this and realize that we cannot change one thing by being stressed or worried, we must turn our eyes to the provisions God has made for us. We must trust in the Word of God with the confidence that there is nothing too hard for the Lord (Jer. 32:17).

Why should we trust in God? Scripture tells us that "The earth is the Lord's, and the fulness thereof; the world, and they that dwell therein" (Ps. 24:1). Genesis 1:1 declares, "In the beginning God created the heaven and the earth." It was God who created everything, and He controls everything, even down to the atom. He decides what atoms will come together to form a molecule and whether tissue will come together to form systems in our bodies. He determines the position of the eyes, the nose, the ears, and every internal organ in the body so that it will function perfectly.

When God made the heavens and the earth and everything in it, He did it by simply speaking it into being and arranging it according to His directives. He put everything in its proper place so that there would be no doubt about the function of each particular thing. If God did this with all that He created, how much more will He, by His Word, direct our lives and provide all that we need to walk in daily victory over stress? We know that we can trust God for this because He sent His Son to shed His blood, pay the price for our infirmities, and bear our stress—our griefs and sorrow (Isa. 53:4).

The birds of the field do not stress; they do not worry, yet they eat daily. We are not able to change even one strand of hair on our heads by worrying, and it therefore behooves us to not be stressed or anxious for anything. But how do we, in practical terms, receive relief from stress, as the birds know it? As we alluded to earlier in this chapter, we must learn to relax. We may be able to do this by going for a walk, looking at birds, playing with our children, or volunteering our services for those in need.

We must take time each day to focus only on God as we read His Word. This daily exercise should include thanking God for everything—even for the negative things, the bad things—in our lives. Of course, our thanksgiving will express appreciation for the beauty of everything God has done, and even the things He is going to do. It is our privilege to thank Him for His promises and for all His goodness.

In the busyness of our daily lives, we must remember to worship God by enjoying all that He has created. For example, we often see flowers and say, "Oh, they are so beautiful." Yet, we seldom take time to bend over and smell the fragrance and appreciate the true beauty because we are so busy passing by. The flowers declare, "I am so wonderful. I am so beautiful. I am God's creation. Will you take time with me?" These words express the glory of God that is present in so many things God has made. However, if we rush and push through the day, we never appreciate the wonderful things that are right at our fingertips.

Relief from stress and worry comes as we determine to quickly dismiss any offense or hurt that comes against us. To do otherwise—to allow it to continue in our system—will cause long-term damage. Paul said it best in Philippians 4:6: "Be careful for nothing; but in every thing by prayer and supplication with thanksgiving let your requests be made known unto God." We should not worry about anything; instead, we should give everything to the Lord and allow Him to deal with it. The result, according to verse 7, is that "the peace of God which surpasses all understanding shall keep your hearts and minds through Christ Jesus."

In Philippians 4:8, Paul continued with encouragement for us to focus not on the negative but on the things that are honest and good. We cannot keep any junk, any hurt, in our hearts if we, as Philippians 3:10 says, want to "know [Christ], and the power of his resurrection, and the fellowship of his sufferings, being made conformable unto his death." We cannot know the power of God that was revealed in Christ's resurrection if we hold onto offenses that will cloud our vision of Him. We will not be able to fully experience those things He set in motion for us when He died for us. If we are blinded and cannot, through faith, see what God has for us, we will entertain those things that come against us and deal with them on a continual basis, day after day. We will go after things that the Lord does not intend for us. But if we understand that God is the source of everything we receive, then we will focus on Him and not on the things that cause stress. We will not be bogged down by offenses and blockades, hurts and pains that come to us.

Then we will reach for those things that are before us, not looking back, not taking time to even focus on the things behind us. We will join with Paul, who said in Philippians 3:14, "I press toward the mark for the prize of the high calling of God in Christ Jesus." We will press for that mark and strive for it because there is nothing else we really need to work for. As we focus on Christ and His goodness, we can let go of the past and forgive those who have hurt us so deeply. As we allow the Lord to minister to us, we can be free. We are set free when we completely release our offenses and hurts.

As we take these steps, the Lord will allow His angels to come and minister to us. He will give us new hearts with a new love that surpasses all understanding. It will keep us walking in peace day after day. Material things will not be important. What people say may hurt, but it will not stay with us because love will overcome all hurt and pain.

Stress is not for the believer. We who are believers, called by His name, are victorious according to 1 John 5:4. We are victorious and we overcome the world by our faith. We must put our faith into action and tell God, "Lord, I believe You. I believe You can take these pains, these hurts and put them under Your blood, which You shed for me. I believe You can take everything that has occurred to me, and, Father, I receive Your total help. I voluntarily release my stress to you. I hold onto it no longer."

I encourage you to make this your prayer for deliverance from stress and your declaration of Christ's victory over it:

Jesus, this day I give You all my problems, all my concerns, all my worries, everything that has ever plagued me, that has ever bothered me. I give it to You freely now this day, Father, never to be bothered by it again. I give You all my enemies. I give You every concern. Lord, I place them at Your feet, and, Lord, I will not pick them up again, because I cannot handle them. I cannot deal with them. But You can, Lord, so I voluntarily give them to You and thank You for taking them, for I know that You are my Lord; You are my God. You paid the price on Calvary, and I thank You for it this day.

I am stress free. I am no longer bound by things of my past, things that have tormented me for years, because I know that You are not a God of torment, nor a God of fear. But You are a God of more than enough. You are a God who is able to supply all my needs according to Your riches in glory, and it is Your good pleasure to do that. And freedom and peace of mind are the things that You delight in giving me. I know that You desire that my soul prospers, and that I be in good health. Therefore, this day, I am prosperous, I am in good health, and my mind is free. I have no stress, no worry, no concern, because You are my Lord and You are my God. I take my rightful place as a King's daughter. I take my place in the royal priesthood to be free to go and come as I please without shackles or bonds or any type of restriction. I am truly free this day.

I thank You for the miraculous. I thank You for the open door. I thank You for being my Lord, and I thank You for being my God. For truly You are worthy of all the honor, all the praise. You are worthy. You are the King of kings and the Lord of lords, and I invite You to come into my heart and into my mind in a special way this day as You so deem. You are like a breath of fresh air, and I thank You for the newness. I thank You for the newness in my heart and in my spirit. I thank You for who You are in my life this day. Even though I have loved You for a long time, I thank You for a new beginning in You today, because You are El Shaddai. Thank You.

12

GENERATIONAL CURSES

A GENERATIONAL CURSE IS essentially a negative attribute or trait that is passed down from one generation to another. A generational curse is an offense that hovers around one who has not participated in it, waiting for a chance to manifest itself. This happens because whatever one does can be passed on to one's children, grandchildren, and even great-grandchildren. God described generational curses this way:

> And the LORD passed by before him, and proclaimed, The LORD, The LORD God, merciful and gracious, longsuffering, and abundant in goodness and truth, Keeping mercy for thousands, forgiving iniquity and transgression and sin, and that will by no means clear the guilty; visiting the iniquity of the fathers upon the children, and upon

> the children's children, unto the third and to the fourth generation.
>
> —Exodus 34:6–7

It is hard to believe that one's way of life will affect someone possibly for hundreds of years. This can be good or bad depending on the acts that one does. It is good if there are generations of faithful, loving fathers and mothers who care for their families and are excellent role models for their children and the community. However, it is sad to watch the actions of one who is disrespectful, loud, or abusive be repeated in the first, second, third, and even fourth generations. This can be true of alcoholism, gluttony, and drug addiction, not to mention fear, divorce, adultery, and suicide. The list goes on and on.

We must be careful about the thoughts we think in our minds and the deeds we do with our bodies. If we were to prayerfully consider the effect on future generations, we would not contemplate or do certain things. We must guard not only our physical bodies, but also what we think. The thoughts we entertain can open the door to fantasy, which leads to sinful actions.

Many of us do not want to accept the blame for our children's shortcomings. It is much easier to say that their actions follow the choices they have made. While that is true to a certain extent, Exodus 34:7 teaches that the deeds of the parents are passed down even to the fourth generation. The only way it can be stopped is to allow the blood of Jesus to prevail in our lives and in the lives of our children.

Principles of Generational Curses

Where did generational curses begin? When God made Adam, the first man, and breathed the breath of life into him in Genesis 2:7, He gave him authority and power over the world He had created. However, Adam lost that authority, or rather he gave it to the devil when he sinned in the Garden of Eden. Generational curses started at that point, when Adam yielded to sin and surrendered the authority God had given him. Romans 6:16 says, "Do you not know that to whom you present yourselves slaves to obey, you are that one's slaves whom you obey, whether of sin leading to death, or of obedience leading to righteousness?" (NKJV).

We become a servant to whomever or whatever we allow to manipulate us or work through us. If we yield ourselves to sin, we are servants of the devil. If we yield ourselves to righteousness, we are servants of the Lord. Many times we surrender the authority Christ has given us in the spiritual realm and cause succeeding generations to have turmoil because of it. For example, we lose authority in our bodies and allow sickness and disease to afflict us. We do not take the proper authority and power that Christ has given us to declare that we are well, we are healed, we are delivered, and we are free.

A vicious cycle of good and evil began after the fall of man in the Garden of Eden. When Cain killed Abel, a generation of evil was established. Because of his spirit of jealousy and murder, "Cain went out from the presence of the Lord" (Gen. 4:16), and he and the ungodly line that came from him were cursed from that time forth. But then the Lord gave Seth to

Adam and Eve in Genesis 4:26, "And then began men to call upon the name of the LORD."

The Bible is faithful to describe the effect of generational curses, and one example is seen in the story of Eli, a priest who committed gluttony (1 Sam. 4:18). As a result of his lack of discipline, his sons Hophni and Phinehas had other addictive problems. They were deceptive and stole from the people of God, and they were also sexually promiscuous with the women who served at the door of the tabernacle. Even though Eli talked to them, he never did anything to stop them from their evil ways. First Samuel 4:11–18 tells how the Lord punished both Eli and his sons. Another example is that of King David and King Solomon. David sinned with Bathsheba, and his son Solomon repeated his father's sin by allowing himself to be led astray by foreign women (1 Kings 11).

As these stories show, a generational curse may manifest itself in a different sinful behavior in the following generation. Sometimes, however, the curse is repeated exactly as the generation before. A nine-year-old girl from a small town delivered a healthy baby in a hospital in a larger town nearby. The girl's mother was eighteen years old; her grandmother, twenty-seven; and her great-grandmother, thirty-six. As long as the family could remember, the mother had her first child out of wedlock at nine years of age. This generational curse was hopefully stopped with this young lady, who received extensive counseling.

I believe that certain spirits travel with other spirits. For instance, wrath, bitterness, fighting, and brawling can be a generational curse when a spirit of anger takes over. And a spirit of control tends to go along with a generational spirit of bitterness. People who are tormented with a spirit of control and a spirit of bitterness want to be at the top and control every situation. They want to dictate what is to be done and where and how. They further desire that their opinion should be superior to all others. No one else should have the right to dictate what is done and when it is done.

Another "partnership" of spirits that travel together is the spirit of gossip and the spirit of discord. These generational spirits pay no attention to the truth of what one person says about another. It just has to be juicy. The spirit of gossip tends to carry along a spirit of procrastination—not being able to do things in a timely fashion, putting things off to the last minute, making excuses for why something is not done.

People who are tormented by the spirit of gossip and the spirit of discord tend to always want an assignment, and they are resentful of others who have an assignment. However, when they are given an assignment, they will not fulfill or complete what they were asked to do. We must guard against this and be careful to stay on task and follow through on the assignments God has entrusted to us. We must not be envious or desirous of anyone else's role or anyone else's authority. Rather, we must be satisfied with the assignments we already have.

Christ's Deliverance from Generational Curses

How should we respond to the spirit of generational curses? We must accept Isaiah 53:4–5 as truth and understand that "surely [Christ] has borne our griefs and carried our sorrows" when He died on the cross. Surely He has taken our sicknesses, weaknesses, distresses, and woes. He was bruised for our guilt, and our need to obtain peace and well-being was upon Him as He died. He has already paid the price for our every need.

We must also know that Jesus' death on the cross provided deliverance from generational curses. This deliverance is given only by request, and all we have to do is ask for it. If we, according to Romans 10:9–10, confess the Lord Jesus with our mouths and believe in our hearts that God has raised Him from the dead, we will be saved. We must believe that Jesus is who He says He is, the Son of God; that in His death He was punished for every sin we could ever commit; and that He rose again with all power in His hands. We must repent of every sin we have done against Him and acknowledge that Jesus is truly Lord, able to deliver us from generational curses.

I would like to share three stories that describe God's ministry of deliverance from generational curses. First, a young man began to dabble in witchcraft and traced his involvement back to his great-great-grandfather, who was considered a great warlock and had great powers. Although the young man called on the power of evil for a time, he eventually called on the name of the Lord and was saved and delivered.

In a second instance, a man's daily, excessive drinking was passed down to all six of his children, who also drank daily from the time they got up until the time that they went to bed. His grandchildren—all except two of his daughter's twelve children—followed suit. Many of them died of liver disease, enlarged hearts, heart attacks, and strokes. But his two grandchildren who did not drink began to call on the name of the Lord, and their turning toward God extended to their cousins. They had searched in vain for satisfaction in alcohol, and God gave them life, joy, and peace in the Holy Ghost through Christ Jesus.

Finally, a mother who had a problem with sexual promiscuity passed this sinful lifestyle down to her daughter and granddaughters. The granddaughters, understanding that this was a generational curse, sought the Lord about it and helped the previous two generations, who were still struggling with their flesh at their older ages. Only because the younger generation called on the name of the Lord did deliverance come to this family.

13

DEATH

ALMOST THIRTY YEARS ago, I experienced something that has followed me all my life. I became a Christian in the third grade after losing my father when I was in second grade. I loved my father, and like all little girls I felt he could do no wrong. He taught me about the Lord and His goodness.

My dad told me, "Be the best of whatever you are going to be. If you straddle the fence you are no good to anyone." He also said, "If you are going to be a devil, be the best one you can be, but if you love the Lord, then do all you know to do to serve Him and please Him. Be the best Christian you can be as well as an example to others."

I followed my dad everywhere he went. Never did I tire of listening to him or being at his side. My dad was the epitome of love and kindness. He always had a gentle word for all and was generous to a fault. He said that tears should not be wasted or used for persuasion or manipulation but only for the deepest hurt. Because tears are precious, they should be used only if they are sincere, even when death occurs.

My dad, who was almost twice as old as my mom, died at the age of seventy-one. I did not cry at all except at the graveside. I had to shed one tear. Daddy was worth that and many more, but for some reason only one would come. Since that time, I have cried much because I miss him so. I understood that he had to go. Even though I was so young, he prepared me well for what was about to happen to me in my lifetime.

The next year I gave my life to the Lord. I asked the Lord to show me if He was real and to come into my life. As I dedicated my life to the King of kings and Lord of lords, I saw a light come into the church. No one else saw it, but it was so bright, so grand, that it consumed all the darkness. From that time on I prayed every day petitioning the Lord to help me to be what He wanted me to be.

I began to see visions and have dreams at an early age. I had a vision that my mother's best friend had died, even though she had not been sick. A few minutes later the phone rang and my mother was screaming and crying that her friend was, indeed, dead. I prayed and asked the Lord to take these visions and dreams from me. He did until I became a teenager, and the gifts returned then, stronger and more vivid than ever.

A Conversation with Dr. Death

As the years passed, I continued to love the Lord and pray to Him. I went to medical school and was in the lounge one day wasting a little time before classes. Usually the room was filled with people, but that day no one was there but me. The door opened, and suddenly the room turned cold as a man about five feet, seven inches tall walked in. I immediately noticed his hair because it was thick and sandy with the coarseness of wool. His skin was bronzed and weather-beaten, while his eyes were red like fire. His face had massive, distinct scarring, almost as if someone took time to etch lines with vivid clarity and purpose into his face. Each line and scar seemed to tell a story. Some of the marks, even the scratches, seemed very old, while others seemed deep and fresh.

The man talked as if he were on crack or cocaine, speaking each word with speed and accuracy and making eye contact after every other word. He wore hospital scrubs, green ones, in fact, which were ironed to perfection, and had tennis shoes on his feet. As he was speaking, he wrote Greek and Hebrew on his hand. The writing was very neat, almost as if a computer were writing it into book form.

"I know you," the man said. "Your name is Gloria Johnson." As I listened in amazement, he told me my life story. "I have seen many men die, many men die," he continued. "In fact, I have just left the operating room, and he died. But you will be a great surgeon one day. I have been in many battles, many battles, and seen many men die, but you will be a great surgeon one day. I was in this battle and that battle, and many men died; but you will be a great surgeon one day. I was there when Grant died, I was there when this one died, then the other, but you will be a great surgeon one day. You will go through medical school, and you will be in many battles, but you will be a great surgeon one day."

He talked to me for twenty to thirty minutes telling me what

I would do in life and how I would be victorious in life over and over again. Then he became specific about some things that would occur. He continued to write in Greek and Hebrew and looked at me with those cold, red eyes, which appeared to show eternity as well as the ages of time past. I could literally see in a vision the wars, the battles, the dead he had seen as he walked through history. It was like someone was narrating pictures that were being shown by a projector.

Finally, the man stood to conclude, "You will be a great surgeon one day."

Although I was amazed at what was happening, I was not afraid at all. I asked him, "How do you know me and all these things about me?"

He looked deep into my eyes and asked, "Don't you know me? Gloria," he laughed, "don't you know who I am?"

Following him to the door of the student lounge, I replied, "No. Who are you?"

"I am Dr. Death," he said.

As soon as he closed the door, I opened it. However, no one was in the hallway. As my friends began to enter the lounge, I told them what had happened. We searched the building and the campus and looked at all the employee pictures. However, no one had seen the man except me. The campus police searched and searched in vain and even watched the dorm.

As time went by, I knew I would see Dr. Death again someday, some way, even if others did not. I talked to many people about that conversation, but the Lord gave the interpretation as well as the understanding of it. The death angel had come to acknowledge the Christ in me because I would win so many battles against him through the blood of Jesus. The passing of years has confirmed the truth of this.

The Power of the Christ in Me

We have been given the authority to bind death because of the Spirit of the Lord within us. It has been my joy to participate in God's victory over the death angel, and I would like to share some stories of God's power and His compassion for His people.

One time, a patient was dying on the operating table. The Lord had instructed me to fast and pray before surgery that day, and when I went into the room and saw the patient struggling, the Lord said, "Lay your hands on the patient." Immediately, he recovered.

A fellow physician was going to give birth to a premature baby who was not expected to survive. If the baby did live, the high-risk team was available with oxygen and all the necessary equipment to help with respiratory problems. We held a prayer meeting in the room with the nurses and doctors before the surgery, and the baby was born with no need for oxygen or any medical assistance. Everyone was amazed, but they all knew it was truly the Lord's doing. A physician who had turned away from the Lord after her brother was killed during gang violence rededicated her life to the Lord after that, glorifying Him for what He had done.

When a man's heartbeat stopped, his wife looked at me and said, "I just can't let him go, even though I know I should." After we laid hands on him and petitioned the Lord together, he not only revived but also lived a very good life for almost five more years. God gave him a clear mind, and he walked with a cane and did his regular work around the house. When he became ill again, his wife said to me, "I know he is tired. I can let him go now." Peacefully, without struggle, he passed away within a few days.

One experience that is very dear to me happened when my oldest sister died. She told me, "I think the Lord is going to take me today, but if He does it is OK. I am ready." Even though she had not even been feeling bad, she immediately became ill without warning and grew progressively worse over two days. We rushed her to the hospital to find that she had massive pulmonary emboli. I did not leave her except to go to the bathroom because I knew the death angel was in the room. I knew he could not steal my sister while the Christ in me was in the room.

I stayed with my sister until she was declared stable and then left just to take a bath. However, while I was in the shower, I felt a kiss on my cheek. Immediately I knew that the death angel had won the battle. My sister was dead and she had kissed me goodbye. I quickly returned to the hospital with the intention of praying death from my sister. But as I arrived it was as if the sun had set in the room, and the most beautiful smile on her face said, "I am happy now."

The Spirit of the Lord spoke to me, "Would you want to return from that?"

"No, Lord," I replied.

"Then leave her alone," He said.

Instantly a mountain of peace from God came upon me as I had never experienced before. It surpassed all earthly or natural understanding.

I faced the death angel again when my nephew became very ill and was hospitalized. He, like his mother whose death I just described, had pulmonary emboli, and the doctors said he would probably not live. His heart rate was greater than two hundred and his blood pressure was also elevated. I saw the death angel enter the room, and even though I was pregnant, I did not leave my nephew's side. I continually prayed and petitioned that God would not allow him to be taken. After about twenty-four hours, all his vitals miraculously normalized. Even his doctors said, "We can't take credit for this one; it had to be God." After five years, my nephew is still living.

The Lord will not allow the death angel to take one of His children until that person's loved ones can tolerate it. To that end, the Lord gave certain rights and keys to us as believers. He holds the keys of hell and of death (Rev. 1:18), but He has given us the keys to bind and loose on earth and in heaven (Matt. 16:19). Many don't exercise the power and authority that Christ has given to us. As we become believers we automatically inherit the keys, but it is up to us to use the keys to unlock the doors.

A Near-Death Experience

In 1998, Robert William Kelly of Gahanna, Ohio, was on a Caribbean cruise with his wife when he began to have a terrible headache. His wife was worried and said she did not want him to die, but he felt that she was overreacting. However, he did give in to her and went to his doctor when they returned home. Although the doctor thought Robert had nothing to worry about, he continued to have headaches and an MRI revealed a mass on his brain. It turned into an aneurysm after it was pinpointed, and he underwent surgery.

Although he was expected to be in the hospital only a few days, he remained unconscious for over a week. During this time, while his wife sat next to him praying and watching for some type of sign that he was about to be better, Robert went on an adventure. It started in darkness that was darker than he had ever seen before and it got darker and darker. As he struggled to fight off panic, some type of light appeared in the midst of the darkness, and he felt drawn to it. As he got closer and closer to the light, his fears and confusion decreased even more.

Robert felt like he was walking through some type of tunnel and sensed a warm, soothing breeze blowing at the back of his neck. It urged him along, and the light became brighter and brighter, gradually pushing him through the darkness that he previously saw. Then he stopped because he felt he had gone as far as he should. He sensed, not saw, that someone else, a young boy, was there with him looking at the same light that he was. And then he heard a voice say, "Uncle Rov, what are you doing here?"

It was his nephew, who had never been able to pronounce his name correctly. He had died of leukemia four years before, when he was only five. Robert called to his nephew and asked him if he was all right, and he said yes. Then Robert's nephew asked why he was there. He told Robert that his wife and children needed him.

Then someone else came along and joined Robert. He saw a young woman who was very beautiful with golden hair moving gently in the breeze. Her dress was white with flashes of gold, and it reflected against the light. After Robert's nephew said good-bye to him and left him alone with the lady, she gave him a smile full of total peace and confidence, and he waited for her to say something to him. However, all she did was smile, and then everything was black again.

The next thing Robert knew, he was back in the world, or at least above it. He was looking down at his body as it lay on the bed hooked up to machines. A nurse was taking a reading, and he saw his wife sitting by herself, tears running down her face. He heard a voice call to him from the distance and say, "Don't worry." It was the voice of the woman he had just seen. She was still with him.

Robert moved to the room where his son, David, was sleeping with his favorite stuffed animal. Then he went to his daughter's room, where she, too, was asleep. She had kicked herself out from under the covers. His nephew was right, he thought. He didn't belong in the presence of the Lord yet. He needed to be with his family. "Please, God," he said within himself, "let me go back to my family."

And then the scene changed again. Robert was back in his hospital room looking down at the scene there. The nurse was gone, and his wife was at his bedside talking to him. "I have to return. They need me," he said.

And then he realized that the lady with the golden hair had stayed by his side and had been guiding him from scene to scene, place to place. She spoke to him again, saying, "You are right; they do need you, and you will go back to them. But you have to understand it won't be easy. That's why I am here."

Everything went black again, and the next thing Robert remembered was being in the hospital bed and looking at the face of his wife, who was overjoyed that he had regained consciousness. Since returning to life on Earth, he has admitted that he has spoken to the mysterious woman many times. He says that he has even seen her. She tells him the same thing she told him when she was with him: his place is with his family. They need him.

God's Angels Were Waiting

The angels of God play an important role when people die. This is vividly shown in "Faint and Break," an article that tells a wonderful story of a ten-year-old girl named Becky and her father, Don, who loved each other very much. Becky was her father's helper and wanted to go with him everywhere he went. They always found joy in each other's company and were essentially inseparable.

"Faint and Break," which is found in *Angels on Earth*, describes what happened one evening in April 1997 when Don, his wife, Terri, and Becky were on their way home from a trip to visit Terri's parents in Fayetteville, Arkansas.[1] As they traveled on a two-lane highway, Terri, who normally was wide awake, became very sleepy. She checked on her daughter, who was securely buckled into her seat right behind her father, and thought, "She'd follow him to the ends of the earth." Then, as she continued to drive, she finally gave in to the sleep.

When she awakened, she saw the most amazing thing. The car had stopped and they were in a sea of fog. Beyond the fog were two persons, it appeared, with halos of light around them and a beautiful, elegant white staircase. Becky and her father, Don, were wearing long, white robes and they were walking hand-in-hand toward the stairs. "There they go again," she said, wondering where they were going. Soon they started up the staircase and disappeared into the mist.

As this happened, she remembered her husband getting up to leave the van and her daughter saying, "Daddy, wait for me." As her husband and Becky walked toward the stairs, she heard a voice say, "Don't worry about where they are going. Just know they are OK and you will see them again."

Terri woke up in the hospital. Her mother was there, and she told her that a van had crossed over into their lane and had met them head-on. Her husband and daughter were gone. Then Terri realized that she had seen two angels standing at the staircase waiting for her husband and her daughter to climb the ladder to eternal life. She remembered the words, "You will see them again," and had comfort in knowing that they were in a better place. They were together and she would see them again.

PART III

HEALING FOR SPIRITUAL BROKENNESS

14

OUR COVENANT RELATIONSHIP WITH GOD

NOW THAT WE have identified specific ways the enemy attempts to steal, kill, and destroy in our lives, it is important that we open our hearts and minds to learn of God and His provision to heal our spiritual brokenness. Since our spiritual brokenness is the result of our broken covenant relationship with God, we will begin this section by discussing the importance of this relationship.

A covenant is a binding agreement between two or more parties. The fact that it is binding means that the agreement will continue no matter what happens to one of the parties. A contract, which is usually used in business agreements, is not always binding. It can usually be broken. We usually look at a covenant in a religious sense. Unfortunately some marriages are viewed as a contract, rather than a covenant.

The Bible tells how God made a covenant with Abraham:

> And when Abram was ninety years old [God had

> not yet changed his name to Abraham] and nine, the LORD appeared to Abram, and said unto him, I am the Almighty God; walk before me, and be thou perfect. And I will make my covenant between me and thee, and will multiply thee exceedingly.
>
> —GENESIS 17:1–2

God reminded Abraham of who He was and commanded him to walk before Him and be perfect. He was not talking about how Abraham walked physically, but about his spiritual walk before Him. Although this wasn't the first time the Lord had spoken to Abraham, He was reminding Abraham of the promises He had made to him, beginning in Genesis 12:1–3. He was telling Abraham that He could not give him what He had promised unless He saw a certain walk. Therefore, He made a covenant, an agreement, with Abraham.

Sadly, the people of Israel, the nation God raised up from Abraham, failed to keep the covenant He had made with them. In Numbers 14, after Israel's repeated disobedience to God, He told the children of Israel, "I have to breach my promise. I have to break my covenant, because you did not do what I told you to do." Numbers 14:34 says, "After the number of the days in which ye searched the land, even forty days, each day for a year, shall ye bear your iniquities, even forty years, and ye shall know my breach of promise."

Just as the children of Israel suffered brokenness in their covenant with God, some of us have a broken relationship with the Lord. We are very upset with Him because He has not done what we feel He should have done. "Lord," we say, "I have prayed and prayed, and, Lord, I have walked uprightly before You. Yet, You have not done what I have asked You to do." We may go to church every time the doors are open but still be broken and angry with God because He has not heard our prayers.

We may suffer a sense of brokenness in our covenant relationship with God, just as Job did. Job 1:1 says that Job was a perfect and upright man and stayed away from evil. And yet, as we noted in Chapter 6, Job lost his livestock, his children, and finally his health, all "without cause" (Job 2:3). It was in this setting that Job wondered, "God, what in the world is going on?" Some of us may question Job's integrity; we may believe that he had to have done something wrong. However, Job 1:22 makes it very clear that Job did not sin or charge God foolishly.

As we also mentioned in Chapter 6, Job could have become bitter, but he decided to wait on God and trust in Him. At times his heart was filled with questions about the way it seemed God had forsaken him, and this seemed all the more difficult when his friends were criticizing him. Yet, he opened his spirit to hear God's words to him in Job 38–41. As he did this, he realized how insignificant he was and how great the Lord truly was. He repented of his wrong thoughts and feelings toward God and forgave his friends. In the end, the Lord restored his health and even blessed him more abundantly than before.

Causes of Our Brokenness

Brokenness in our covenant relationship with God has resulted in many areas of brokenness, which are expressed through a variety of life experiences. For example, we suffer brokenness when a family member or friend dies. Brokenness occurs many times in families for a wide assortment of reasons. Because of adultery—the unfaithfulness of both husbands and wives—many men and women who sit in our churches and serve in places of ministry are in a state of deep brokenness. Sometimes a marriage partner may turn to a homosexual lifestyle and afflict his or her spouse and other family members with brokenness.

Bitterness is consequence of refusing to forgive one who has brought brokenness into a person's life. It is possible for the offending person to confess his wrongdoing and also for the offended person to say, "I forgive you." However, if unforgiveness remains in the human heart and one's heart and mind return to the offense day-in and day-out, bitterness will result. You know that you have forgiven someone if you do not react at all to what that person has done to you. That's total forgiveness.

Some may ask the question, Can we forgive a person's offense when we have not forgotten it? The reality is that we as humans have memories and we are not going to forget painful wounds that have happened until the day we die. However, through forgiveness, sometimes we can look at one who has deeply hurt us and smile. It doesn't even bother us. Other times we may have a flashback and be ready to seek vengeance. We must, by

God's grace, learn to respond like Jesus relates to us. He could remind us of all the years we've done wrong and all the things we still do wrong each day. However, He forgives us.

We are able to forgive this way as we kill our flesh. The more your flesh is killed, the more we are able to forgive what another person has done to us. We have to make the flesh die until our spirit man is stronger than the flesh man. This comes only through fasting and prayer.

Abuse is a cause of brokenness in our lives. It may be expressed through dishonor and disrespect. Division, which I described as "di-vision" in Chapter 7, also brings brokenness. This happens in marriages and families, in churches, and at workplaces. It results in chaos and confusion. The answer to division is for us to submit to God's plan as He has revealed it to us in His Word. This is something I learned after my husband and I were married twenty-seven years ago.

The weekend after I got married, I started to plan a trip from our home in Iowa City, Iowa, to Minnesota to see my girlfriend. When I told my husband, he responded, "Oh, no. You is married now."

I said, "Huh?"

"You can't just get in the car and go to Minnesota," he repeated.

"Well, my mama told me I could do what I wanted to do," I insisted.

"Uh-uh. It don't work like that," he declared.

Even though I was saved and I meant to do right, I struggled with my husband's negative response to my travel plans. God knew what was happening in my heart, and He began to wake me up every morning at three o'clock. He took me right to Ephesians 5:22, where it says, "Wives, submit yourselves unto your own husbands, as unto the Lord." I said, "Uh-uh," and closed the Bible. Three o'clock the next morning I got up and tried to read the Word. Guess where it flipped open. I tried to turn to something else, but it went straight to Ephesians. "No, God," I countered.

This happened every morning for two weeks until finally I gave in to the voice of God and said, "OK, Lord. Forgive me."

Then I went to my husband and said, "Baby, please forgive me. I've been wrong. I tried to overstep what you said. I tried to overstep your authority. Please forgive me. I'm so sorry."

He looked at me and replied, "That's all right."

God's Love Is the Remedy

> Therefore being justified by faith, we have peace with God through our Lord Jesus Christ: By whom also we have access by faith into this grace wherein we stand, and rejoice in hope of the glory of God. And not only so, but we glory in tribulations also: knowing that tribulation worketh patience; And patience, experience; and experience, hope: And hope maketh not ashamed; because the love of God is shed abroad in our hearts by the Holy Ghost which is given unto us. For when we were yet without strength, in due time Christ died for the ungodly. For scarcely for a righteous man will one die: yet peradventure for a good man some would even

> dare to die. But God commendeth his love toward us, in that, while we were yet sinners, Christ died for us.
>
> —ROMANS 5:1–8

Love—not just any love, but the love of God—is the remedy for the brokenness that has come to our covenant relationship with Him. Romans 5:1 describes the work of God's love so well when it says, "Therefore, since we are justified (acquitted, declared righteous, and given a right standing with God) through faith, let us [grasp the fact that we] have [the peace of reconciliation to hold and to enjoy] peace with God through our Lord Jesus Christ (the Messiah, the Anointed One)" (AMP).

Because of God's love, we have an entrance into His grace, His unmerited favor. We are restored to a covenant relationship with Him. Even though we have trials and tribulations, heartaches and pain and disappointments, we are to be happy. We are to rejoice in the hope of God's glory when our money is short, when people disappoint us and say all manner of evil against us, even when we do things to cause ourselves to take a step backwards and get frustrated.

Tribulations work patience in our lives. Every time we go through heartaches and pain, we grow a little bit stronger. As we come to one hurdle, the Lord gives us the strength and the courage to jump it and then, by endurance and patience, continue on to the next. Patience is something that we want yesterday. We grow tired of going through tribulations when it seems like everybody else is getting blessed. It seems the people who mistreat everyone have all kinds of nice things, and we are lonely, wishing for the good things they have. Yet, as we are patient through these times, we grow stronger and gain experience.

Experience qualifies us to warn others about spiritual danger. We can tell them that we have been through the place where they are trying to go and explain that we would never want them to have to deal with the things we have gone through. A man who has been instantly delivered from thirty-one years of crack and cocaine does not want anyone else to have to go through the torment he did. A person who has been delivered from alcohol doesn't want anybody else to suffer with it.

We must learn to be patient as we wait for God to deliver His blessings to us. One person once told me how the Lord blessed him with so much because he was faithful in tithing. The Lord is not going to allow you to do more for Him than He does for you. This is something we learn through experience. The enemy will trick us with the lie that we can't tithe because we have too many bills. However, as we believe and obey God, giving faithfully to Him, He will wonderfully bless us. We have to learn to be obedient to the Spirit of Christ.

As we experience the work of God in our lives, we also have hope. To have hope is to have expectation of something you have not seen. It is just like a woman who becomes pregnant and is expecting a child. She anticipates the joy that will be hers after the baby is born, and it is a joy that is so much sweeter, so much greater than any pain she could experience. This is why the Bible says that once a mother gives birth to her baby, she remembers her pain no more (John 16:21). When she looks at her baby, the blessing God has given her, she doesn't consider the pain she went through.

That's the way it is with experience. After a while you know that whatever you go through is worth it because what God is going to do is so wonderful. Romans 5:15 reminds us, "And this hope does not make us ashamed; because the love of God, is shed abroad in our hearts." In other words, we're not disappointed because God's love is poured out in our hearts through the Holy Ghost. When we were so weak, with no power or strength in ourselves, Christ died for us.

We knew that we needed to be righteous, we needed to be saved, but we didn't even have strength enough to call on the name of Jesus. Yet, God showed His love for us by the fact that Christ died for us while we were still sinners. As Paul wrote in Romans 5:7, it is not probable that very many of us would die for anyone, even if the person were living righteously. I know that I have never told anyone I would die for them. But while we were still in our brokenness, even before we thought about God, He was thinking about us. Thousands of years ago, He was loving us for this day. He was healing us for this day. He was giving up His blood for us, for our joy, for our peace, for our happiness, this day.

Yes, God's love is the remedy for our broken covenant relationship with Him. It is the remedy for all the brokenness in our lives, and we gain access to it by confessing with our mouth the Lord Jesus and believing in our heart that God has raised Him from the dead (Rom. 10:8–10). As we are connected to God through faith in Christ, we receive the inheritance He has provided for us. It is an inheritance of lasting joy, the joy of the Lord that we can enjoy because He, in love, paid the price for us to receive forgiveness of sins and healing for our brokenness.

The Place of Blessings

When Jesus died on the cross, while we were still in our sins, He prepared some wonderful things for us. Salvation, of course, was number one, but there are other things that are almost inconceivable. While we were still in our sins, living, as it were, in the gutter, God saw us in tuxedos and evening gowns. He prepared a grand ballroom with everything we could ever desire—the finest chandeliers, the most delectable foods, and the finest company.

The enemy sees how great, how grand all this is, and he wants to keep us from receiving what the Lord has for us. Therefore, he continually sows confusion into our minds so that we will never see some of the things in God's inheritance for us. He keeps us wondering why someone made a negative remark to us or why someone else did an unkind deed.

However, we can choose to listen to God. We can receive all the blessings He has for us because Jesus paid the price for them. Not only can we receive cleansing for our sins but we can also walk in freedom from bondage. We don't have to pay any money, and we don't have to beg. All we have to do is come to Him and be in His presence. He wants to give us more and bigger blessings, gifts, and rewards that are reserved for us.

If we allow offenses to rule our lives, we will be unable to receive all the blessings God has for us. We must forgive those who have offended us and forget past hurts, pains, and disappointments, letting them go as if they never existed. Philippians 4:8 exhorts us to think on things that are honest, just, lovely, and good. We must seek to allow only praise to come from our lips, not complaints, murmurings, and scorn. As we delight ourselves in the Lord, His will becomes our will. We are happy and satisfied with Him alone, and He gives us the desires of our hearts. This is how we can stay in the place of blessing in our covenant relationship with God.

15

HEALING TRUTH FOR BROKEN MARRIAGES

In Part II of this book, we identified specific spirits that the enemy uses in his attempts to steal, kill, and destroy. Our first topic of discussion was lust, and this chapter will respond to this important area of spiritual brokenness with scriptural insight on God's truth and healing for this significant area of need. There is deliverance and great hope for all who come to God with open hearts and a willingness to obey His Word.

When a husband or wife breaks the marriage vows through adultery, it results in negative consequences for both mates. The offending mate feels guilt, and the faithful mate begins to think, "Maybe I am not good enough. Maybe if I had been nicer or had spent more time with my mate, this would not have happened. I must not be satisfying my mate in the bedroom. It is my fault he or she did this." Many spouses retaliate against the offending mate by committing the same act, and the result may be a bitter divorce.

Why do people cheat on their mates? In thirty years of research on this question, I have received the following answers:

- "It's something to do. I know it's wrong, but everybody does it."
- "It's like something drives me, and I can't control it. Even when I don't want it, I still do it."
- "It makes me feel pretty and good about myself for a while, then I feel so torn inside after I commit the act."
- "I get mad at my spouse and just do it; if she would act right, then I wouldn't be in the streets."
- "I have a good wife, and I don't know why I do it because I don't enjoy it. The ladies offer, and it is like I can't refuse it."

Other reasons for marital unfaithfulness are immaturity and lack of affirmation from a spouse. However, greater than all these things, most of those who have been unfaithful have had some type of traumatic experience as children. Some men who fall into adultery were adopted and felt anger, especially toward their mothers. They actually hated women and therefore had multiple affairs because they felt that women didn't deserve or need any better treatment. Some said their parents showed them no affection—hugging, kissing, or verbal expressions of love and affirmation—during their upbringing.

Regardless of the cause for marital unfaithfulness, it always results in the offender suffering a cycle of guilt, depression, and an increase in the intensity of the sinful act. The act is followed by a period of remorse and then, after a short time, a repeat of the act. This leads to more and more affairs, which consume the offender until he or she admits the problem and truly repents.

No one wins in marriages that are violated by marital unfaithfulness; both parties suffer. However, if a husband or wife, through prayer and supplication, seeks the God of our salvation, the miraculous can and does happen. Many times, God will show the faithful spouse changes that need to occur in the marriage. For instance, effective communication is the key to any good marriage. If one spouse punishes the other with silence, it can be a great offense that causes the marriage to decay. And if a couple bites and devours each other with harsh, destructive words, it is just as bad as silence.

After many years of marriage, the husband and wife may grow apart because their life together becomes routine rather than spontaneous. A strong, healthy marriage requires work, devotion, and commitment to understand what the other mate is going through. It calls for the husband and wife to create a quiet, gentle atmosphere in which they express love and kindness both in word and deed, in the sexual relationship and in every other part of their lives.

God's Plan for Marriage

When God instituted marriage in Genesis 2:18–24, He made Adam a male and Eve a female. He did not make two women for Adam, nor did he make two men for Eve. Further, He did not make two males or two females, but He made one man and one woman. If He had intended any other combination, He would have done it in the Garden of Eden.

Matthew 19:4–6 explains that God brings the husband and wife together to become one flesh and then concludes, "What therefore God hath joined together, let not man put asunder." As the husband and wife live together, they are to live according to the exhortation of Ephesians 5:21–33 to submit to one another, love one another, and prefer one another. The husband is the head of the wife, and he is to love his wife as Christ loves the church. The wife is to submit herself to her husband. Ephesians 5:22 gives instruction for the wife to submit in obedience to her husband as unto the Lord, if he is a believer. Colossians 3:18 directs the wife to submit to a husband who is not a believer with the words, "Wives submit yourselves unto your own husbands as is fit in the Lord."

Sometimes the husband may ask the wife to do something that is not of God, that, according to the Scripture, is not fit in the Lord. This may include taking drugs, drinking alcohol as a stimulation, or watching pornographic movies for stimulation. I believe that in the latter situation, the mate who wants to watch the pornography is stimulated by the person in the pornography, not by the marriage partner. Therefore, the mate will never be able to attain the level of satisfaction the initiating marriage partner desires. This is a subtle trick the devil can introduce through pornography.

The Bible teaches that the husband and wife are to please each other sexually. As 1 Corinthians 7:3 says, they are to show due benevolence, due honor, to each other. Neglect and disrespect, which may include open flirtations with another person directly in front of the mate, open a person to the spirit of lust and the resulting lasciviousness. The solution is to obey the wise counsel of God's Word:

> Let thy fountain be blessed: and rejoice with the wife of thy youth. Let her be as the loving hind and pleasant roe; let her breasts satisfy thee at all times; and be thou ravished always with her love. And why wilt thou, my son, be ravished with a strange woman, and embrace the bosom of a stranger?
>
> —Proverbs 5:18–20

First Corinthians 7:4–5 says that the husband has power over his wife's body and the wife has power over her husband's body. They should satisfy the desires of each other as needed. The only time there should be a separation from lovemaking in marriage is if, by mutual agreement, a husband and wife give themselves to fasting and prayer. A wife should not fast without permission from her husband and vice versa. If either mate has needs, the husband is to satisfy the wife and the wife is to satisfy the husband.

Hebrews 13:4 says that marriage is honorable for all and the bed should be kept undefiled. God has given the married couple the marriage bed as the place to enjoy sexual pleasures by being innovative and keeping things fresh and alive through variation that does not move out of the auspices of the Bible. Mutual sexual satisfaction in marriage helps to deter the spirit of lust, which leads to lasciviousness. Refusal to satisfy one's mate sexually is an open door for the devil to enter one's marriage.

It is fit to do all that a marriage partner asks one to do as long as it is not biblically wrong. It is not wrong for one mate to ask the other to cook or to clean or to make love at any time, whether it be in the morning, at lunch, or at dinner time. This is reasonable service. In marriage, we are to serve one another and care for the needs of the other. We must learn to communicate about our individual needs so that we know how to satisfy our marriage partner.

Both the husband and wife need affection from each other, as well as a healthy sexual relationship with each other. Many times, men who discover that they have hypertension will go without their hypertension medicine because it may cause them to be impotent. Men sometimes feel they are less than a man if they cannot perform sexually for their wives. Meanwhile their wives are telling them, "I just love you, and if you hold me, it will be good enough."

If the husband and wife do not receive the affirmation they need from each other, they feel, "I am not satisfying. I am not pretty enough. I am not attractive enough. I am not sexy enough." To receive the approval and affirmation they desperately need, a husband or wife may go to another person of the opposite sex. Regretfully, this not only happens in the world but also among believers, who may cover their tracks instead of truly repenting.

First Timothy 5:8 says, "But if any provide not for his own, and specially for those of his own house, he hath denied the faith, and is worse than an infidel." If a husband and wife do not care for the needs of each other spiritually, emotionally, physically, and sexually, the Bible says that they are worse than those who do not believe. However, when a husband and wife pray together, they can learn from God how to meet the wants and needs of each other. This happens because they, through prayer, come to have a spirit of unity in their marriage.

We know that there is great power in unity because of what God did in Genesis 11:5–9. When a group of people who were not God-fearing had one mind to build the Tower of Babel, God Himself said, "I cannot stop them because they are one" (author's paraphrase). Therefore, He came down to scramble their language so that they would not have the strength of unity. When there is a spirit of unity in one's marriage, no demon, no devil can stop what God has for that husband and wife.

First Corinthians 7 tells both the husband and wife to stay with each other and live together peaceably, without bickering or arguing or fussing and fighting. It also says that if an unbelieving mate chooses to leave, the believer is to let that person go. He or she is no longer bound to that covenant. Sometimes, a believing husband or wife prays for an unbelieving mate a long time and that person does not change. It is not because God is not God but because that person is refusing to submit his or her will to the will of the Lord.

Significant Biblical Principles

We must never feel that we are too old to be tricked by the devil or so devout that the devil does not have something lustful he wants to offer us. David had been secure as king for approximately twenty years when he was tempted to commit adultery with Bathsheba. The Lord had blessed him with all manner of riches, and everything he wanted was at his fingertips.

Second Samuel 11 and 12 tell how David took matters into his own hands. Not only did he take Bathsheba, the wife of a man who was loyal and faithful to him in all ways, but he also murdered that man, Uriah the Hittite. He then took Bathsheba and married her. The child born from David and Bathsheba's adulterous relationship died, even though David fasted and prayed, vehemently crying out to God to spare the child's life. David also had to deal with the sword of rebellion when his own son Absalom raised against him. Even though God did forgive David's sin with Bathsheba, the punishment, agony, and pain David endured was very severe.

Proverbs 5:1–14 warns men that they must guard against being deceived by the lips of an immoral woman. It shows that a woman or man who is seductive leads foolish people to a place of eternal destruction. Proverbs 7 talks about the wiles of a harlot, a woman who decks her bed, perfumes her bed, and prepares to entrap the "simple" male (v. 7). It describes how she is very subtle and, through persistent flattery and seductive talk, will cause one who is not careful to yield to her enticement. This lustful spirit has cast down many and caused many to go astray. Many who said they were strong men and would never give in to lust have succumbed to it.

The warning of Proverbs 6:27 is so true: "Can a man take fire in his bosom, and his clothes not be burned?" Can one handle lust and escape the destruction it causes? Will it not cause pain? Will it not cause one to go into lasciviousness?

It is true that the Lord forgives the sin of immorality when a person has a repentant heart. As a result, some people may look at others and say, "Well, this person got away with his sin." However, they do not understand the price that person has paid because many times he has not told them.

One example of the horrible price of adultery is seen in the story of a man whose one-time act of unfaithfulness stole a lifetime of reputation from him. He was in his sixties, had always been faithful to his wife of over forty years, and loved and adored her and his family. However, when he was approached by a young lady who was ready to sell her body for some money, he succumbed to her for no earthly reason. As soon as the sexual act was completed, he felt a burning sensation in his genitalia and realized that he could have contacted AIDS or another sexually transmitted disease.

He immediately sought to commit suicide because he knew he could never tell his wife. He felt that he would rather kill himself than disgrace his family. In addition, he was a prominent deacon in one of the local churches and did not want to disgrace his church. When the man went to his private physician for testing, he learned that he had a disease and was able to take medication to cure it. As he cried out to God, he repented with godly sorrow, according to 2 Corinthians 7:10.

Even though God forgives the sin of marital unfaithfulness when there is repentance, the consequences of it cannot be sidestepped.

> But whoso committeth adultery with a woman lacketh understanding: he that doeth it destroyeth his own soul.

> A wound and dishonour shall he get; and his reproach shall not be wiped away.
>
> —Proverbs 6:32–33

These verses apply not only to man, but also to women. God's gift of salvation is so wonderful and great that we must guard it and refuse to look at the sexual allurement of one who is not our marriage partner. It is not worth letting down our standard for a moment of pleasure that produces a lifetime of misery.

We must shun the very appearance of evil and stay away from people or things that would entice, even if we have to close our eyes. To increase our strength against evil, we can daily read the Word of God and renew our minds.

> I beseech you therefore, brethren, by the mercies of God, that ye present your bodies a living sacrifice, holy, acceptable unto God, which is your reasonable service. And be not conformed to this world: but be ye transformed by the renewing of your mind, that ye may prove what is that good, and acceptable, and perfect, will of God.
>
> —Romans 12:1–2

As we daily crucify the sinful tendencies in our bodies and our flesh, our spirit man will grow and come to rule and dominate our very being. As we seek to please God in all things, our lives will have a demonstration of righteousness that comes not from our human efforts to follow the Law, but from Christ's transforming power at work in us.

Through repentance and surrender to God, we are made

free from sin. Now, we must obey Paul's exhortation, "Stand fast therefore in the liberty wherewith Christ hath made us free, and be not entangled again with the yoke of bondage" (Gal. 5:1). We must refuse to go back to sin and allow it to take control in our lives again. Because we are in Christ, we are no longer under condemnation and we "walk not after the flesh, but after the Spirit" (Rom. 8:1). We are conquerors over sexual sin because we live and thrive on things of the spirit. Romans 8:6 says, "For to be carnally minded is death; but to be spiritually minded is life and peace."

God calls all people to repentance. It is for everyone. If we repent and confess our sins, we have the promise of 1 John 1:9 that God "is faithful and just to forgive us our sins, and to cleanse us from all unrighteousness." He is faithful and just, willing and happy and pleased to forgive all our sins. Even more than that, He will restore that which was taken from us in a greater measure if we simply love Him and serve Him.

This is possible because Jesus paid the price for every sin when He died for us at Calvary. No matter how devious, how deceitful, how treacherous our sins may be, the Lord has already provided forgiveness. Once we turn our hearts and minds toward the Lord and ask Him to wipe away our sins, including the sin of lust, He does. Isaiah 53:4 says, "Surely he hath borne our griefs, and carried our sorrows."

A Lesson from the Life of Solomon

Solomon, the successor to King David, was a great man, a wonderful man, who loved the Lord. In 1 Kings 3:4–15, God appeared to him in a dream and asked him, "What would you like me to give you?" Instead of asking for riches and houses and lands and concubines, Solomon asked for wisdom. God was pleased by Solomon's response, and He blessed him not only with wisdom that surpassed even the eldest person but also with all the riches of the land, the finest of jewelry, gemstones, and houses. He gave Solomon such honor that even the Queen of Sheba came to see him and was amazed at his wisdom and all that he had (1 Kings 10:1–13).

God allowed Solomon to build a wonderful temple of worship for Him. In spite of this, however, Solomon failed to heed God's caution to love Him and walk in His ways, to keep His statues and commandments (1 Kings 3:14). Even with repeated warnings from the Lord, he made the same mistake others had made before him and married women who were idol worshipers (1 Kings 9:1–9; 11:1, 9–13). He mixed his love for God with the spirits of those he married because he had sexual relationships with them. First Kings 11:4 says that his wives turned his heart after other gods.

Because this happened, Solomon came to a state of emptiness, a state of illusion that God really was not who He said He was. He came to the point where he said, "All is vanity, all is empty, there is nothing that means anything, nothing that will suffice, nothing that is so important." Essentially, he was saying, "I really do not worship God, everything is empty, there is no fulfillment in God for me any longer because of the infiltration of the spirits of these idol gods." All this happened because of Solomon's lust for his many foreign wives.

But Solomon's story has an excellent and a beautiful ending.

As Solomon turned back to the Lord and reached out for Him, he came up with this beautiful conclusion:

> Let us hear the conclusion of the whole matter: Fear God, and keep his commandments: for this is the whole duty of man. For God shall bring every work into judgment, with every secret thing, whether it be good, or whether it be evil.
>
> —Ecclesiastes 12:13–14

In Ecclesiastes 12:1, Solomon advised the youth, "Remember now thy Creator in the days of thy youth, while the evil days come not, nor the years draw nigh, when thou shalt say, I have no pleasure in them." He warned them to leave youthful lusts alone and look instead to the Lord.

As we consider the brokenness that the spirit of lust causes in so many marriages, we must receive Solomon's wise counsel. We must shun and stay away from those things that are not of God because they will lead us to a place we really do not want to be. We must repent of sins that have separated us from God, receive His forgiveness, and be transformed by His power to live in healthy marital relationships.

16

RECEIVING HEALING THROUGH RELEASE

The previous chapter pointed us to the power of God's truth and healing for the spirit of lust. This chapter will identify specific ways God ministers healing for several other areas of brokenness we may suffer because of spiritual evil that is directed against us. I believe it will be a source of encouragement and hope for you to see how we receive healing as we release our deep pain and wounds to God.

Release from the Spirit of Bitterness

In Chapter 6, we recognized the very destructive force of bitterness, not only for oneself but also for others. Bitterness can literally kill us. Yet, God is able to deliver us from the control of the spirit of bitterness so that we can enter into the release God has for us. As long as we are still alive, we can choose to respond to bitterness by searching for the one and only living God, the Lord Jesus Christ, who releases us through His blood, which He shed for us on the cross.

This happened for a woman who was torn apart with bitterness and suspicion toward men for over seventy years. When she was a young girl, she was violently raped by a man who knew her family well. The man warned her that he would kill both her and her mother if she told anyone, and she kept the secret until she was eighty-three years old. As a result, she grew up bitter and distrusting of all men except her dad. She felt that every man would attempt to hurt every young girl and therefore developed a paranoid attitude toward men.

After suffering physical abuse in her first marriage, which ended when her husband left her, she married an older man who was twice widowed. At first she thought of him as a father since he was almost twice her age. However, after taking her to the grocery store or wherever she needed to go for a season, he asked if he could "come courting." She said yes, and they began a wonderful love relationship that surpassed all she had ever known. He was a wonderful husband, and to her surprise, at almost forty years old she had three girls.

Because of the rape she had suffered many years before, she warned her daughters to never let a man see them undress. Also, she always thought the worst of every man who came around her daughters. Although she loved her husband, she still had a fussing spirit. He could not quite get things right for her. Her husband was once unfaithful with an older lady, and on his dying bed he confessed and asked to be forgiven. She gladly forgave him and remained a widow the rest of her life.

She was generous to a fault, even to give her last to those in need. She would take strangers off the street and be kind to them. Feeding them with the little she had was nothing to her, and she would say, "The Lord will always provide." She lived in a small house all her life, but after her children were grown, they, to her surprise and satisfaction, purchased a house for her. Even with all that she had been blessed with, including her relationship with the Lord, something on the inside of her was still tearing her apart. When she was finally able to confess the rape that had happened to her as a young girl, she felt that a load had been released. Her whole attitude both about life and the people around her changed. Release from the spirit of bitterness is so important for our health.

Choosing to Release Our Offenses

All of us suffer offences, and the solution to them is simple yet complex. It is simple because all it takes is letting go of the offense in our minds. It is complex because it is not easy to release something that may have enslaved us for many years. If we are able to totally ignore an offense, we have no problem or stress and therefore no need for intervention. This can only be accomplished by a focused mind.

Every time an offense comes to mind, we must rebuke it and deny that it has any further hold. We must think on the pleasantries of life, the pure things, the honest things, and the things that lead to a path of joy and peace. The blood Jesus shed on the cross two thousand years ago is strong enough even now to deliver us from any problem or offense we have suffered, no matter how long ago it happened. Jesus has already paid the price for the solution, and now His arms are wide open to receive us.

As we take our offenses to God to receive His deliverance

and healing, we must release them to Him. This means that we choose not to receive hurt or pain or to hold on to it but rather to take hold of that which gives life. To release offenses we have suffered is a voluntary action. We must refuse offenses, decline them, and vehemently object to them. How we cope with life's problems determines not only our well-being, but also our progression to the specific destination God has for us as individuals.

We can think of God's plan for us as a course that is outlined for a train. The purpose of a train is to transport passengers safely to their destination. As long as the train is not derailed, it should reach its intended place by a specific time. But if it is derailed, detained, or stopped, it may never reach its destination. It may never fulfill its purpose. In some cases, due to the many deformities resulting from wreckage (offenses), the train could become nonfunctional. In other words, although the destination may be reached, the train may be disabled and no longer able to fulfill its purpose of safely transporting passengers.

It is very important that we consider God's purpose for us and respond wisely to any offense that has derailed us from the course He has set for us. Many of us suffer from offenses beyond our control, things that happened when we were children, teens, or young adults. Some problems may be the results of generational curses and others may have happened because we failed to obey the voice of the Lord in very practical areas of life. Regardless of our ability to understand why offenses occur in our lives, we must choose to listen to God as He speaks to us through His Word, and we must obey Him.

The Power of Intercessory Prayer

Many who have suffered the very destructive effects of offenses have received God's deliverance and healing as they have turned to God and His ministry through the power of intercessory prayer. For instance, one man who had been delivered from cocaine, alcohol, and cigarettes for five years fell back into bondage to these things. In fact, his addiction was greater than it had been the first time. He found himself wanting to commit suicide, and he continued to decline until he was at his worst state ever. When he asked the body of Christ to offer intercessory prayer for him, deliverance came.

In another example, a woman who had been in the church for over thirty years had weathered many trials in her marriage to an unfaithful husband who threatened to kill her because she went to church. After he died, she thought her life was stable. However, a friend she had known and prayed with for over twenty years betrayed her, and it devastated her. Even though her friend, who truly loved the Lord, was sorry and begged for forgiveness, the woman could not get over the pain of betrayal, no matter what she did. The woman began to feel sad all the time because she allowed the hurt to linger. She cried without reason, found no joy in anything she did, and began to sleep all the time. She lost her appetite and eventually could no longer cry. A spirit of depression had entered her life through an open door, and she remained in a depressed state for almost two years. Although she did not even have a mind to pray and could not pray for herself, she was delivered after much intercessory prayer.

A third example is the story of a man who had been delivered from many spirits, such as stealing and fornication. He married a lovely lady who adored him and loved the Lord, working faithfully in Christian ministry. However, after a lingering disagreement with his wife, he opened the door to adultery, lasciviousness, and stealing. After raping a prostitute in an act of rage and violence, he became extremely afraid that he could no longer control himself or his emotions. The man would leave home for days without calling to say where he was, and he would curse his wife if she asked where he had been. Finally, he realized that he must make a change. He admitted that he was unable to focus his mind to pray, and through the intercession of others he was able to receive deliverance. He and his family were restored to each other, and he began to value his peace in the Lord.

In a final example of the power of intercessory prayer, a woman who was an evangelist and the head of a corporation was very well educated and mild mannered. She very rarely got upset with anyone, and most people thought that she prayed all the time. One day, however, one of her employees disregarded her spoken wish and the woman became enraged to the point of planning to kill her employee. She could not rid herself of the thought no matter what she did, nor did she have a mind to pray at all. She was about to execute her plan when a lady who knew her called and said that the Lord had told her she needed prayer. In response to this intercessory prayer, the evangelist was delivered not only from anger, rage, and murder but also from lustful thoughts, which had first opened the door of her spirit to evil.

Release from the Effects of Stress

As I mentioned in Chapter 11, persistent stress can weaken us to spiritual attacks that come against us through destructive afflictions such as depression, cancer, and fear. The good news is that God, through the shed blood of Jesus Christ, has provided release and deliverance from these things. One instance of this happened in the life of a woman who had been involved in multiple affairs with married and unmarried men but had come to the point where she wanted to settle down and find comfort and peace in her life.

This woman felt that she had met someone who would be with her the rest of her life, even though she was not married to him, but all of a sudden he walked away. To really make things worse, one of her children had contracted a deadly disease and was continuously using drugs to mask the pain that came with it. In the loneliness of trying to support her children and the mental anguish of having to deal with all her failures, she decided that it was too much. She wanted to end it all and just take her life. She felt that she could not pray or read the scriptures because she didn't think that the Lord would hear her after all the wrong she had done. But she did turn to the Lord and call upon Him. As she did, the depression began to leave. And as she prayed to Him and read scriptures each day, the Lord touched her mental abilities. The Lord delivered her as she began to give focus and attention to the Lord and the good things in her life.

In another example, a woman developed cancer after suffering many years of heartache and disappointment. Her husband, who was bitter and angry, essentially felt that his life was over and that she was useless to him. Therefore, she went around trying to make everyone else happy, even though she was not happy herself. She tried to live her children's lives for them and assisted them in every way she could. Because she essentially neglected herself, she developed high blood pressure and also had to have a pacemaker put in. She finally reached the point at which she really wanted to die because she felt that was the only way she could receive rest from all the things she was dealing with. Various family members were so unhappy, and she felt that she could do nothing to help them. She worried continually, trying to pay the bills and satisfy herself and her family members.

It was in this stressful state of life that this woman developed cancer. It was a fast-growing, very malignant cancer that was expected to end her life within a few months of its diagnosis. She began to call on the name of the Lord, and together with a friend who also knew the Lord, fasted and prayed. Within three days, a repeat study was done and the bone marrow test showed that no cancer was present. The doctors could not understand what had happened. Why would this cancer disappear? Why was it gone? The woman God had healed simply told them, "Because I am a child of the King, and my Daddy has done His work again."

PART IV

BLESSED WITH ALL SPIRITUAL BLESSINGS

17

THE BOTTOM LINE

EPHESIANS 1:3 GIVES us the wonderful promise that God has "blessed us with all spiritual blessings in heavenly places in Christ." In the remaining pages of this book, we will consider some of the ways God gives us these gracious blessings. The first thing we want to examine is the bottom line of God's plan and purpose for our lives.

It is vital that we look beyond our circumstances and focus our hearts and minds on Christ and the end He desires to fulfill in us and through us. We must make it our goal to get to the core, the center, of His revealed will—a growing, intimate covenant relationship with Him. This means that we will need to learn both what God wants for us and also what we need to do to progress in our steps toward Him. What will it take for us to go where God has called us? And what will it take for us to stay there?

We introduced God's will for us to have a covenant relationship with Him in Chapter 14. At the beginning of that chapter, we looked at Genesis 17:1–2 and its description of God's covenant relationship with Abraham. In this chapter, we will step back to the verses that first introduce us to the covenant God made with Abraham:

> Now the LORD had said unto Abram, Get thee out of thy country, and from thy kindred, and from thy father's house, unto a land that I will shew thee: And I will make of thee a great nation, and I will bless thee, and make thy name great; and thou shalt be a blessing: And I will bless them that bless thee, and curse him that curseth thee: and in thee shall all families of the earth be blessed.
>
> —GENESIS 12:1–3

Abraham came from a pagan society in which he and his ancestors were idol worshipers. However, God called him to separate himself from his people and the idol worship in which he was involved. God told Abraham that He had something for him, but he could not receive it where he was. He had to leave his pagan background and go where God was going to show him.

Today, God calls us to separate ourselves from spiritual darkness and bondage into the light and freedom of a covenant relationship with Him. He does not want us to walk in agreement with those who are bound by Satan in the destructive works of the flesh. In fact, He even asks us, "Can two walk together, except they be agreed?" (Amos 3:3) The devil, on the other hand, wants us to be content to walk in agreement with those who are in bondage. He knows that if we are walking in victory and freedom, we are going to influence others to walk in victory and freedom.

God calls us to separate ourselves from agreement with sin and evil because He has something He wants to give us. God told Abraham, "If you will separate yourself and come out from among your people and their pagan worship, I will make you a great nation. I will bless you and make your name great and wonderful, so that everyone will know that it is I who blessed you." In other words, God said that He would put Abraham's name up in lights. Even though Abraham's enemies hated him, they would have to respect the fact that Abraham was blessed and honored by God.

Further, God declared that Abraham would be a blessing to others. He would not be selfish, but giving. When we receive something, we must be careful that we do not hold on to it and keep it all to ourselves. We may be tempted to hide a blessing we receive and say, "I got it, Lord. I don't have to tell anyone." However, we are to bless others with what God has given us.

God promised Abraham, "I will bless them that bless thee." When someone gives us something, God wants us to put it in His hand. He, in turn, gives it back to the person who gave to us. Perhaps the blessing we receive is a kind word, a prayer, a cold drink of water, a sweet potato, a piece of meat, or a dime. Whatever it is, God will bless the one who gave to us. God wants us to walk so that the blessings we receive from others will roll back to them as a blessing.

Yes, God is pleased when we look for opportunities to bless others. That, in fact, is what we are here for. I remember the blessing I received when a young man in my neighborhood came and prayed with me to give his life to the Lord. That's what it's all about. I had been praying for the neighborhood for years. Every time I drove down the street, I cried, "Lord, save them; save all of them." I would stop the car and ask, "How ya'll doing?" I would talk to them a little while, being careful not to beat them over the head with the Word.

When we show others a little love, we can gain them as brothers and sisters in Christ. That is what made me so happy when that young man stepped out of the destructive works of darkness and came into Jesus. Now he is discipling his whole family and he wants to preach. God is working in his life to help him deal with issues from his past and also to prepare him to meet the requirements for ministry in Titus 1:5–9.

In addition to promising a blessing to those who blessed Abraham, He also said that He would "curse him that curseth thee." If someone curses us, God will deal with it. We may be tempted to take the matter into our own hands, but we can trust God to minister His righteousness and justice on our behalf. God is Lord over blessing and cursing, and He told Abraham, "In thee shall all families of the earth be blessed."

Delivered to Abide in the Joy of the Lord

> When the unclean spirit is gone out of a man, he walketh through dry places, seeking rest, and findeth none. Then he saith, I will return into my house from whence I came out; and when he is come, he findeth it empty, swept, and garnished. Then goeth he, and taketh with himself seven other spirits more wicked than himself, and they enter in and dwell there: and the last state of that man

> is worse than the first. Even so shall it be also unto this wicked generation.
>
> —Matthew 12:43–45

In Chapter 2, we talked about this teaching of Jesus, which describes a man who was delivered from an unclean spirit. Because he was still an empty house, the unclean spirit returned and brought seven more wicked spirits along to once again inhabit the man. This shows the importance of seeking God after we are delivered. We will not be able to walk in victory over evil if we, as Amos 6:1 says, are "at ease in Zion." We must not allow ourselves to become so comfortable that we fail to go to God in prayer.

Sometimes we go a little too far with the very thing the Lord delivered us from. Because we are clean and feel good about it, we start peeping at things we shouldn't. For instance, it can seem that a delicious oatmeal cookie is actually calling out to one who looks at it with a desire to eat it. We each have one or more areas of spiritual weakness, our "cookies," as it were. You know what your cookie is. It talks to you when you look at it. You may escape and run, get a little strength, but you come back the next day.

Now if you touched the cookie the first day, you heard it call you, why are you going to go back again? You know that it is going to say, "Eat me, eat me, eat me." And then you are going to say, "Maybe just a little piece." That's all it needs—just a little peephole. It's like being in a rural area and going into a barn where you can see little rays of sun coming through little bitty holes. The holes aren't big enough to put anything through them, but you can squint with your eye and see everything that is happening outside.

That's the way it is with demons. They, like light coming through a peephole in a barn, only need a little hole to step back into our lives. The result is that we are in a worse state than when we started off. We may blame it on our husband or wife or someone else. However, the truth is that it is strategically planned by the enemy, who does not want us to walk in freedom and keep our joy in Christ. He works to reenter our spiritual houses if there is an opening.

If the devil can steal your joy and your peace, he will offer you an oatmeal cookie. He will offer you the destructive works of the flesh in place of joy. However, as Nehemiah 8:10 says, "The joy of the LORD is your strength." Nehemiah 6:15 tells how the Jews, with the joy of the Lord as their strength, overcame much opposition to complete the rebuilding of the walls of Jerusalem in less than three months. In the same way, we can overcome the enemy of our souls by the strength that is ours through the joy of the Lord. We can learn to abide in the joy of the Lord by rejecting the negative counsel of friends who would drag us down and by honoring God with hearts of thanksgiving for His many blessings to us.

It is so important that we keep our joy. We must not let anything or anybody steal it. No husband can make his wife lose her joy, and no wife can make her husband lose his joy. No situation can make us lose our joy if we have a connection with the Lord, a relationship with the Lord. We as individuals choose if we will have joy. We can have it 24 hours a day, 7 days a week, 365 days a year because we have the King of kings and the Lord of lords living in us. We have relationship with the One who can heal and deliver us.

Fear God and Do What He Says

In Chapter 15, we learned an important lesson from the life of Solomon. We learned that we must shun and stay away from things that are not of God. We must repent of sins that have separated us from God, receive His forgiveness, and be transformed by His power so that we can find fulfillment in a growing, intimate relationship with God.

Beginning with his marriage to Pharaoh's daughter, Solomon made the mistake of marrying women who were idol worshipers. His wives turned his heart after other gods, and it got to the point that he felt that life wasn't worth anything. Ecclesiastes 2:1–11 tells how he tried to find satisfaction in wine, folly, the finest of houses, vineyards, riches, and much more. Yet, it meant nothing, because he had lost God. He had lost the very thing he was seeking: his relationship with the Lord.

Finally, however, God showed him the conclusion of the matter, the bottom line. He showed him, as Ecclesiastes 12:13 says, that the only thing that matters in life is to "fear God, and keep his commandments." That's it. Fear God and do what He says. We have to stop justifying wrongdoing and understand that the Lord is looking for righteousness. Because of God's grace we have tasted of His goodness, and we are called to walk uprightly before Him. We are to embrace the Lord with everything we have and love our neighbors as we love ourselves.

In Ecclesiastes 12:14, Solomon reminds us, "For God shall bring every work into judgment, with every secret thing, whether it be good, or whether it be evil." God sees everything we do—our attitudes and the deeds we do in our bodies—and He is going to deal with all of it according to His righteous judgment. This applies to every secret thing, whether it be good or evil, for what we do in the dark will come to the light.

The bottom line, then, is that we have to do life God's way. We can make ourselves comfortable with what we're doing our way, but when we come down to it, it still has to be His way. We can spend forty years doing things our way and justifying that somebody made us do it that way. But when we are really honest about it, we will acknowledge that no one can make us do anything. Yes, the bottom line is that we have to do what God says.

18

FULL DELIVERANCE

SINCE THE BOTTOM line is that we are to do life God's way, it is vitally important that we receive full deliverance from the power of spiritual evil. Many people wonder how they can be fully released from spiritual struggles that began in their childhood and continue to torment them. How should they deal with the pain and suffering that has followed them throughout their lives? To answer these questions, we will go to the prophet Jeremiah and his hope-filled words to the Jewish people who were being held captive in Babylon.

In Jeremiah 29:14, God gave His chosen people the precious promise that He would turn away their captivity and bring them back to their homeland. However, as verse 10 says, this would not happen for seventy years. It was important for the Jewish exiles to receive God's truth that they had to face their present consequences because they had rejected the God who made a covenant with their forefathers Abraham, Isaac, and

Jacob. As a result of their hardened hearts toward God and their refusal to respond to Him with faith and obedience, they had been driven away from the land He had given them.

In addition, since the Jews were, in fact, going to remain in Babylon for seventy years, they were to pray for the city where they were living and give of their lives to seek peace for it (Jer. 29:7). They were to recognize as deceptive the prophets who said their stay in Babylon would be brief (vv. 8–9). It is natural that we want to hear things that will make us feel good. However, it is so important that we face the truth and deal with it. Everything we do will have certain consequences, whether we want to believe it or not. Just as He did with the seventy years of Jewish captivity in Babylon, God has a set time for the things in our lives. In response to this, we must trust in His thoughts and words, which bring peace.

> For I know the thoughts that I think toward you, saith the LORD, thoughts of peace, and not of evil, to give you an expected end.
>
> —JEREMIAH 29:11

In this verse, God is saying, "I know what I'm thinking toward you. I have good thoughts to bless you, to bring you to a place in Me, a place in the Spirit, a place of peace and joy. However, you just don't want to see it. I have caused you to be scattered, to be cast in one direction and then another, because I am trying to bring you to the place that I know you can be. I am not trying to make your life miserable. I'm not trying to make you suffer or hurt or do without. If you will allow me to, I will bring you to the place of peace."

God's thoughts are to give us an expected end. In other words, He is trying to bring us to a point of being in a good position. We can all improve, no matter who we are or what our title is. Many times we walk around with a smile on our face but have multiple skeletons in the closets of our lives. When someone asks, How are you? we say, "Oh, praise the Lord." Yet, all the while, we may be angry at others.

> Then shall ye call upon me, and ye shall go and pray unto me, and I will hearken unto you.
>
> —Jeremiah 29:12

This is God's answer for full deliverance—"Call upon me." When we call on Jesus, we need to put our struggles and concerns in His hands. We must be careful that we do not dictate how He should work and move. Instead we must allow Him to bring changes according to His plan, even though we may not like how He does it. God will bring about change, and it will reveal His goodness and bring glory to Him.

God knows what it will take to bring us to the place where we cry out to God with a heart that sincerely desires change. When we get desperate enough, we will stop what we have been doing and turn to do something else. We will look for a true answer instead of a temporary solution that is just going to make us feel good for a little while. We are tempted to look to sources of financial help that can rescue us from the consequences of our sin. However, the Lord has a way of cutting off those sources, and He will do it to get us where we need to be.

We must examine our hearts to see if we really want to change. When we get desperate enough, we will fall on our face and say, "Lord what is it? How do I need to change? What do I need to do? Lord, I'm desperate." If we're still playing with our bondages, if we still have a hidden agenda when we come to God, we're not desperate enough yet. If we are still doing things our way, still pouting or getting mad, we're not ready yet.

The Fruit of Fasting and Prayer

Fasting and prayer is one way we may express our desperation for God to change us. However, even when we fast and pray, we must come to God with an honest, sincere heart. We must be aware of the deception that may be lurking in the shadows of our hearts.

> Wherefore have we fasted, say they, and thou seest not? wherefore have we afflicted our soul, and thou takest no knowledge? Behold, in the day of your fast ye find pleasure, and exact all your labours. Behold, ye fast for strife and debate, and to smite with the fist of wickedness: ye shall not fast as ye do this day, to make your voice to be heard on high. Is it such a fast that I have chosen? a day for a man to afflict his soul? is it to bow down his head as a bulrush, and to spread sackcloth and ashes under him? wilt thou call this a fast, and an acceptable day to the Lord?
>
> —Isaiah 58:3–5

Sometimes, we may afflict our souls but see no change. We may starve ourselves and lose a few pounds but still find ourselves doing the same ungodly things as before. Even when we are fasting, we may steal and lie and not treat people right. Instead of relating to others with love and kindness, we may think only about ourselves—"I, I, I; me, me, me." We may use the Word of God harshly against people in need because we have gained no knowledge or understanding of God's Word and His way in our fasting. We may learn things about God but fail to come into the true knowledge of God. This is not the kind of fast God has chosen for us. He calls us to fasting and prayer that is so much more than a religious exercise in which we afflict ourselves. If we do not come to God in a true fast, we merely draw attention to ourselves by having our heads bowed down and spreading sackcloth and ashes under us. As Jesus said in Matthew 6:16, we have received the reward of man but no heart change or deliverance from God.

> Is not this the fast that I have chosen? to loose the bands of wickedness, to undo the heavy burdens, and to let the oppressed go free, and that ye break every yoke? Is it not to deal thy bread to the hungry, and that thou bring the poor that are cast out to thy house? when thou seest the naked, that thou cover him; and that thou hide not thyself from thine own flesh? Then shall thy light break forth as the morning, and thine health shall spring forth speedily: and thy righteousness shall go before thee; the glory of the LORD shall be thy reward.
>
> —ISAIAH 58:6–8

The fast God has chosen is one that produces practical expressions of Christ's love and care for those who are bound by the bonds of wickedness and oppressed by heavy burdens. It results in the ministry of providing bread for the hungry and shelter for the homeless. This can happen because a true fast unto God opens our eyes to see ourselves as we really are. God talks to us and tells us what we need to do. He brings us to a place of humility before Him and gives us the desire not to offend others. Fasting that is done in the wrong spirit will be reflected in anger against others.

Fasting that truly seeks the heart of God will bring complete deliverance. People will know that we are delivered because the light of Jesus Christ will be in us and "break forth as the morning." In addition, we will be healthy—healthy in mind, in body, in every part of us. This will come as we examine ourselves and ask God to show us what we need to clean up. We pray, "Give me a clean heart and renew a right spirit within me. Purge me with hyssop. Lord, I want to be right; I want to be whole. Lord, I want everything that is not like you to be gone."

When we fast and pray with a right spirit, our righteousness goes before us and opens doors. I know the Scriptures say that we are saved by grace and not by our works. However, once we love the Lord, we have an obligation to walk uprightly before Him. That righteousness goes before us and is a testimony that God has delivered us. Others see our righteousness, which flows from the life of God within us, and it opens doors for us to minister His life and truth to them.

When God Turns Away Our Captivity

Fasting and prayer with a repentant heart that truly desires to be changed by God shows that we are calling upon Him. We seek God with desperation because we know that He is the only One who can bring about change in our lives. He is the only One who can turn away our captivity. And He even blesses us abundantly with all that we need for the works of ministry He has entrusted to us. I have seen this in many ways, including His provision of rice to send for distribution to the needy in Nigeria and a desperately needed extension of time to renew the license for our secured ministry Web site. God is a wonderful God. He has blessed our ministry, the Cathedral of Prayer in Columbus, Georgia, with the ability to help those in poverty. He is faithful.

> And ye shall seek me, and find me, when ye shall search for me with all your heart. And I will be found of you, saith the Lord: and I will turn away your captivity, and I will gather you from all the nations, and from all the places whither I have driven you, saith the Lord; and I will bring you again into the place whence I caused you to be carried away captive.
>
> —Jeremiah 29:13–14

Do you wonder why some people cannot get delivered, even though they come to the altar time and time again? The answer lies in the measure of desperation they have in their hearts. When we search for God with desperation, with all our heart, we find Him and receive His ministry of full deliverance. The fact that we "find" God does not mean that He has been lost. He has never been lost. Rather, He has always been available. We just haven't been looking in the right places. He's not at the nightclub or in a quart of Haagen-Dazs ice cream. He's not in a woman or a man, but He's in that secret place that only you and He can enter into.

God promised that after He turned away the captivity of the Jews, He would gather them from all the nations where they had been driven. He said He would bring them back to the place He had preordained for them to be. God has extended this word of hope to us as well. Regardless of where the enemy has taken us captive, God is able to take us out of that foreign place of torment and despair. He is greater than the enemy of our souls, and He will bring us back to the place of prosperity and blessings He has provided for us. He does it as we call upon Him in desperation and search for Him with all our heart.

My Personal Testimony

I have personally experienced the importance of being desperate for God and calling on Him. Before I got saved, I was full of me. I was a Baptist but Mama would also take us to the Methodist churches and the Pentecostal churches. I would go up to the altar for prayer and say, "If you've got something for me, let me feel it." I know how people feel when they come for prayer and express that.

When I was about nineteen, a friend who was saved told me about her church. My response was like, "Yeah, right." When I went with her, I was nice to everybody. However, I said, "I just don't take to all that jumping and hollering and stuff."

And every time I'd go up for prayer, folks were falling out. I would go up, but nothing happened. Because I didn't supply anything, I didn't receive anything.

I loved the Lord the best I knew how, and I understood that He was God. I had also read the Bible for myself, and I figured it was wrong for a reverend to go around the church grounds smoking and drinking. I called Mama from college and asked her, "Why does reverend so-and-so smoke?"

She said, "Honey, pray for him."

As I read a little further in the Bible, I noticed other areas of life in which church leaders did not live according to Scripture. When I asked my mother again about these situations, she repeated, "Honey, pray for them. Pray for him." Every time I read something in the Bible, the Lord would open up my understanding. I got to the point that when I walked into church I would say, "Lord, I'm missing something. I don't know what it is, but I know I need something." As I grew desperate for that something and called on God, it didn't take a long time for Him to "whomp" me. "OK," I said. "OK, this is it. This is it."

Before that day, there had been too much of "me" in me. From that day forth, however, my whole life was changed. Everything was new. I've always been a happy person and have always had friends around me, but that day my whole life changed.

19

OUR WALK WITH GOD

And it came to pass after these things, that God did tempt Abraham, and said unto him, Abraham: and he said, Behold, here I am. And he said, Take now thy son, thine only son Isaac, whom thou lovest, and get thee into the land of Moriah; and offer him there for a burnt offering upon one of the mountains which I will tell thee of.

Genesis 22:1–2

In Chapter 17, we discussed Genesis 12:1–3, which first introduced us to the covenant God made with Abraham. The blessings God promised to Abraham were truly great, and one of them was the birth of Isaac, the son God miraculously gave to him and Sarah in their old age. Although Abraham made some mistakes during his life, he repented of them and was called "the friend of God" (James 2:23). He was sensitive to hear the voice of God and then respond to

His change of directions for him. Abraham kept the lines of communication clear in his relationship with God.

One day the Lord tested Abraham to see if He could really trust him with what He had for him. God had blessed Abraham and Sarah with Isaac when Sarah was past menopause. The healthy Isaac was living evidence that God keeps his promises. But God had something even greater for Abraham, a more glorious revelation of Himself than Abraham had yet seen. And so, God gave Abraham the test we read about in Genesis 22:1–13. He instructed Abraham to take Isaac, the only son he had by Sarah, and offer him as a burnt offering on a mountain in the land of Moriah. He told Abraham to kill Isaac, the son he loved. He wanted to see how much Abraham loved Him.

When Scripture says that God tempted Abraham, we must be careful to understand that this means the Lord *tested* him. It does not mean that God tempted him with evil (James 1:13). He does not tempt us with sin or evil because He is not an evil God. When we are tempted to sin, it is because we are drawn away by our own lust (James 1:14). God, however, does test our response of obedience because He wants to take us through a trial that will prove He can trust us to walk with Him on a higher level of spiritual growth and maturity.

Abraham arose early the next morning to do exactly what the Lord had said. Two of his servants came along with him and Isaac, until the third day. Just before Abraham and Isaac continued alone to the place of sacrifice, Abraham told his servants, "We will be back after we go up and worship God." He didn't say, "I will be back." He said, "We will be back."

He prophetically spoke into existence what the Lord God was about to do.

However, Abraham had not told Isaac what the Lord had told him to do. As they walked together, with Isaac carrying the wood for the burnt offering, Isaac asked where the lamb was. "My son, God will provide," Abraham replied. "The Lord will provide the sacrifice." I believe that if Abraham thought Isaac was the sacrifice, he would have said, "Son, you're the sacrifice." But no, he said instead, "My son, the Lord will provide the sacrifice." In other words, "He's going to make a way out of no way."

When they came to the place where the sacrifice was to be offered to God, Abraham built an altar, laid the wood in order, and bound Isaac and laid him on the altar. Just as Abraham was about to slay Isaac, the angel of the Lord called out from heaven and said, "Abraham, Abraham." It is so apparent that Abraham was alert to hear God's voice, for he said, "Here I am." When the angel called Abraham's name, he heard it. The angel told Abraham not to lay his hand upon Isaac to harm him in any way. He explained that Abraham had proved his fear of God because he had not withheld his only son from Him. As Abraham looked up, he saw a ram that had been caught in a thicket by its horns. God truly had provided the sacrifice, and Abraham offered it in place of Isaac. By his trust in God and obedience to Him, he passed the extraordinary test God had given him. And when the Lord was ready to change directions, he was alert to hear Him and receive His blessing.

Called to a Holy, Righteous Walk

> I beseech you therefore, brethren, by the mercies of God, that ye present your bodies a living sacrifice, holy, acceptable unto God, which is your reasonable service. And be not conformed to this world: but be ye transformed by the renewing of your mind, that ye may prove what is that good, and acceptable, and perfect, will of God.
>
> —Romans 12:1–2

God does not ask us to sacrifice our children to Him, but He does call us to sacrifice something. He says that He wants our bodies as a living sacrifice, holy and acceptable to Him. As a living sacrifice, we are not to be conformed to this world, but we are to be transformed by the renewing of our minds. When we are transformed and our minds are renewed in their understanding, we can bring our bodies and our flesh under subjection and walk as a living sacrifice. This is God's perfect will; to do otherwise is to walk in His permissive will.

It is so important that we walk uprightly. In Romans 6:1, the apostle Paul asked, "What shall we say then? Shall we continue in sin, that grace may abound?" In other words, Shall we make excuses about our walk so that increased grace will have to be extended for us? His immediate response was, "God forbid." He was saying, "No, don't do that. Stop." He further questions, "How shall we that are dead to sin live any longer therein?" In other words, If we are truly dead to sin, why are we daily walking in it?

Eleven verses later, Paul taught us how to walk as those who are indeed dead to sin. He said:

> Neither yield ye your members as instruments of unrighteousness unto sin: but yield yourselves unto God, as those that are alive from the dead, and your members as instruments of righteousness unto God. For sin shall not have dominion over you: for ye are not under the law, but under grace....Know ye not, that to whom ye yield yourselves servants to obey, his servants ye are to whom ye obey; whether of sin unto death, or of obedience unto righteousness?
>
> —Romans 6:13–14, 16

No part of us—mouth, eyes, or arms—should be yielded to sin. Instead, we are to use our members to do good things, acts of righteousness unto God. Sin should not have dominion over us. If sin has dominion over us, it has control over us. It has reign over us and compels us to walk in unrighteousness. We crave it, we can't live without it, and we succumb to it. It has power over us, and we are unable to stop it.

Instead of living this way, however, we must remember that we "are not under the law, but under grace." We are not under rules that say, "Don't do this," and "Don't do the other." Rather, the love we have for Christ should be so great that we want to please Him and do what He has called us to do. Sometimes it may be difficult to hear God speak to us, but we must wait on Him. As he did with Abraham in Genesis 22, God will prove Himself and show Himself strong. His blessing and anointing will break the yoke of sin's bondage.

Paul made it very clear that we will be servants to one master or another, either to sin, which leads to death, or to obedience, which leads to righteousness. If we yield ourselves as servants to alcohol, that is our master. If we yield ourselves as servants to sexual promiscuity, that is our master. If we yield ourselves to overeating blueberry doughnuts and Haagen-Dazs ice cream, that becomes our master. All these masters and many more will speak seductively to us and say, "Enjoy me—today."

To walk in sin will lead to death, whether it be natural death or spiritual death. People who have been deep in sin for an extended period of time look dark and have no light in them. Even people who do not know Christ can recognize this. They may say, "There's something wrong with so-and-so. I saw him, and he just doesn't look right. Doesn't he belong to your church?" The people who say this are watching our walk because they really want to stand up and be right themselves.

The Danger of Walking Away from God

When we walk away from God, He expresses His love to us by warning us about the danger of our ungodly choices. He says, "Come on back. You're in a dangerous place." He calls to us like parents who see their children going too close to a busy street: "Come on back; don't go into the street." Just as truly loving parents tell their children when they're wrong and call them back to that which is right, the Lord also warns us about our sin and calls us to come back to Him.

Sometimes it seems as if we can't hear God when He speaks to us about our disobedient walk. And even when we do hear Him as we are in the deepest part of our sinful actions, we may choose to continue in them because we think we do not have the strength to stop. This is a very foolish choice that hinders not only our walk with Christ but also the blessings He wants to pour out on us. And if we persistently walk away from God, we open ourselves to some very destructive consequences.

> Wherefore God also gave them up to uncleanness through the lusts of their own hearts, to dishonour their own bodies between themselves: Who changed the truth of God into a lie, and worshipped and served the creature more than the Creator, who is blessed for ever. Amen.
>
> —Romans 1:24–25

In these verses, Paul describes what can happen to people who reject the clearly-revealed knowledge of God and His glory. When they, because of their hardness of heart, do not repent, God gives them up to uncleanness. He essentially says, "Have at it. Do whatever you want to do. Do it as long as you want to do it, as hard as you want to do it. Go on and do it. I'm moving out of the way. I've called you. I've asked you to stop, and you won't stop. Therefore, go ahead and do all you think you are big and bad enough to do. Have at it, but be prepared to suffer the consequences."

The action of following after uncleanness happens because of lusts of the human heart. As I mentioned earlier in this chapter, God does not tempt us with sin or evil because He is not an evil God. When we are tempted to sin, it is because we are drawn away by our own lust. However, if we let Him, God will take our temptations and turn them for our good according to His promise for those who love the Lord and are the called according to His purpose. He is a compassionate God and has suffered everything we will ever suffer, yet He was without sin. He wants to make our lives into testimonies of His goodness and grace, and He is able to do it.

> For this cause God gave them up unto vile affections: for even their women did change the natural use into that which is against nature: And likewise also the men, leaving the natural use of the woman, burned in their lust one toward another; men with men working that which is unseemly, and receiving in themselves that recompence of their error which was meet. And even as they did not like to retain God in their knowledge, God gave them over to a reprobate mind, to do those things which are not convenient.
>
> —Romans 1:26–28

Because rebellious men and women reject God and His truth, God gives them up to vile affections. Women change their natural sexual relations to that which is against nature, women with women. "And likewise men leave natural sexual relations with women and burn in their lust one toward another." These same-sex relationships, which we call homosexuality, were rampant in Sodom and Gomorrah, the two wicked cities God destroyed with fire in Genesis 19. People who engage in homosexual behavior receive recompense—payment—for their sin.

If people want something bad enough, they will overlook God and the blessings He has put before them and go after something that will never satisfy. When they realize that one thing does not satisfy, they will try in vain to find something else that will. Because they do not like to retain God in their knowledge and respect His instructions, He gives them over to a reprobate mind, a depraved mind. He just turns them over to follow their own evil desires and walk in what they feel is right.

> Being filled with all unrighteousness, fornication, wickedness, covetousness, maliciousness; full of envy, murder, debate, deceit, malignity; whisperers, Backbiters, haters of God, despiteful, proud, boasters, inventors of evil things, disobedient to parents, Without understanding, covenantbreakers, without natural affection, implacable, unmerciful: Who knowing the judgment of God, that they which commit such things are worthy of death, not only do the same, but have pleasure in them that do them.
>
> —Romans 1:29–32

When God gives people over to a reprobate mind, their lives are filled with all kinds of unrighteousness. One of them is murder, and we must beware that we do not murder each other with our tongues. In Psalm 7:15, David described how the wicked "made a pit, and digged it, and is fallen into the ditch which he made." If we are busy killing each other with our tongues, we may end up destroying the work God desires to do in our lives.

Another evil that works in the reprobate mind is backbiting. To backbite is to say one thing in front of a person and something different when that person is not with you. When this happens, it is difficult for the one who backbites to look directly into the face of the one he has been talking about in another setting. If I have something to say about you, I need to say it to your face. We have to love one another and be real in our walk. If we bite and devour one another, we are doing the enemy's job.

To engage in the activities of a reprobate mind is also to be without understanding. The measure of our understanding has nothing to do with our age, for some old folks don't know what they're doing. Rather, understanding speaks of the wisdom that only the Lord can give us. This is an important need in our lives because, as Paul wrote in Romans 10:2, it is possible to "zeal of God, but not according to knowledge." If we understood some things, we wouldn't do some of the things that we do. We wouldn't walk the way we walk.

The reprobate mind results in people becoming covenant-breakers. As we have already discussed, God desires that we walk with Him in a covenant relationship. When we receive Christ as our Lord and our God, we make a covenant with Him to serve Him. Every time we choose to serve someone or something else instead of God, we break that covenant.

At the end of Paul's list of unrighteous actions and characteristics is the adjective *unmerciful*. This can happen in our lives even if we have come to God and received His forgiveness for stealing, murder, adultery, fornication, drug addiction, alcohol addiction, whispering, covetousness, and homosexuality. Even though God has forgiven all our sins, we may be unmerciful in our response to someone who offends us. We may want God to forgive us but not be willing to forgive others. It displeases God if we expect others to be perfect in their response to us while we are unmerciful toward them.

As we conclude our study of this scripture, we must take special notice of a statement Paul made about those who commit the wickedness that flows out of a reprobate mind. He said that they not only do unrighteousness but they also "have pleasure in them that do them." This is not of God. It is wrong for us to get happy when someone else gets in the same mess we are in. God calls instead to enter into true joy and happiness by encouraging others to join us in our walk with God.

Walking After the Spirit

> There is therefore now no condemnation to them which are in Christ Jesus, who walk not after the flesh, but after the Spirit.
>
> —Romans 8:1

God's will for us is that we be released from condemnation by walking not after the flesh but after the Spirit. For this to happen, our spirit man must be strengthened, and our flesh man, with all its desires, must be brought under the control of the Holy Spirit. Romans 8:12–13 puts it this way: "Therefore, brethren, we are debtors, not to the flesh, to live after the flesh. For if ye live after the flesh, ye shall die: but if ye through the Spirit do mortify the deeds of the body, ye shall live." The only way we can walk after the Spirit is to kill the desires and deeds of the flesh.

For us to walk after the spirit, we must, according to Matthew 5:6, hunger and thirst after righteousness so that we will be filled. If we read the Bible and pray to the Lord, a certain spiritual strength comes to us, and we don't even want to do those things we used to do. We don't even have a taste or a desire for evil. The problem is that we don't allow the spirit man to reign in us long enough for us to go out and walk after the spirit. Instead, we allow other things to replace the Holy Spirit and His ministry to us.

Some of us come to God only when we find ourselves in trouble and want Him to help us. We lack the consistency we need so that our prayer will go directly to heaven without any interference anytime we call on God. We fail to understand that our strength comes from lying before the Lord and daily walking and talking with Him. We don't take time to listen to God but go on our merry way and do our own thing if all is going well.

Because we are not walking with God as closely as we need to, we may be deceived by a spirit of error when we think He is talking to us. The effect of this error is that we do not have complete deliverance. When we are completely delivered from something, we don't want to see it again. We don't want to taste it or be bothered by it. The Lord will do this in us if we want Him to. He will do in us whatever we desire. If we want to be delivered and set free, He will do it.

God wants us to be clean vessels, people who walk after the Spirit. The enemy may try to keep us from walking that walk by attacking us with deep hurt and difficult problems in our background. However, if we line up with God the way He desires, He will bless us with growth in our covenant relationship with Him. He may not intervene in our lives or change our circumstances the way we desire, but when we taste and see that He is good, we will want more and more of Him. We will want Him and only Him. We will seek Him with our whole heart.

20

A MAN AFTER GOD'S OWN HEART

And it came to pass, as the ark of the covenant of the LORD came to the city of David, that Michal, the daughter of Saul looking out at a window saw king David dancing and playing: and she despised him in her heart.

1 CHRONICLES 15:29

KING DAVID WAS a man who walked with God and sought after Him with his whole heart. In fact, Acts 13:22 describes him as "a man after [God's] own heart." One of the ways David walked with God was through his worship to God. A highlight of David's worship occurred in 1 Chronicles 15, which tells of the joyous celebration that happened when he and the elders of Israel brought the ark of the covenant to Jerusalem, to a tent he had pitched for it there. The ark, which had been captured by the Philistines in 1 Samuel 4:11 was returned by them to Kiriath Jearim in Israel

(1 Sam. 6:21–7:2). Now, after the entire reign of King Saul and the establishment of David as king, the ark was coming to reside in the capital city of Israel. As Israel's king, David planned an extravaganza of worship for this most significant event. And on a personal level, he danced and praised and worshiped God with all of his might. He thanked Him, magnified Him, and glorified Him.

Why would David do this? I believe it was an expression of worship that flowed out of his heart as he looked back over his life and saw all that God had done in him, for him, and through him. Perhaps he remembered that his great-great-grandmother was Rahab, the prostitute who assisted the spies at Jericho shortly before it fell to Israel. She had repented of her sins and turned to the Lord, and God had saved her and her house. In God's plan, she had married into the line of Judah and became the great-great-grandmother of David.

David was the youngest of Jesse's eight sons. Sometimes people overlook the youngest child, and this almost happened when Samuel went to Bethlehem to anoint one of Jesse's sons as king. Samuel, of course, saw all of Jesse's big, strong, mature boys, and he just knew that one of them should be king. However, God forbade Samuel to anoint any of them and said, "Man looketh on the outward appearance, but the Lord looketh on the heart" (1 Sam. 16:7). God looks at the sincerity of the heart, to see if it yearns to please Him and do the things that are acceptable in His sight.

When David was brought in from keeping the sheep, God told him, "He is the one." With this word from God, Samuel took the horn of oil and anointed David as king. God had chosen a young shepherd boy who was doing what seemed unimportant to some to be king over His people. Many times we may find ourselves doing things that nobody else wants to do. Some may think that God will never use us. However, the Lord is constantly looking at our hearts and the reason we do things. Are our motives pure? Do we do things to be seen or heard by man or for the glory and honor of God?

God has ordained us to fulfill the ministry He has for us. He has put a vision in our hearts and called us to honor and serve Him where He has placed us. We have to know who we are in Christ. We cannot allow people to speak into our spirits and tell us what we can and cannot do. This is when the enemy may try to offer us things that would hinder us from being who God wants us to be. However, we must reject his temptations and distractions and determine by faith to be who God wants us to be.

Memories That Promote Worship

Because King Saul had disobeyed God, an evil spirit came upon him and tormented him. The people around Saul were concerned about this and told him that David, a boy in Jesse's house, could play the harp for him and help him feel better. Thus, David came to serve the king in this way. When David played the harp for Saul, the evil spirit would leave because of the anointing on the harp and its music. David loved Saul and became his armor-bearer.

This is an illustration of the power and authority we have in God's anointing upon our lives. If we through prayer will simply use what God has entrusted to us, no demon in hell can occupy the same space that we occupy. When David stopped playing his harp or when David was not available to play, the spirit would return. But as long as David was playing the harp and allowing the music to flow, Saul could not be occupied by the evil spirit. Our warfare against evil is not carnal; it is spiritual. We do not have to curse or fuss or fight. Rather, we raise our weapons as we are in prayer on our knees, pulling down every imagination of the flesh and spirit.

Then came the time when David slew Goliath, the first of many giants (the others were not physical giants) he faced in his life. Nobody else would go up against Goliath, but the Lord allowed this shepherd boy to kill him by putting a smooth rock in a slingshot and aiming it at the right place. God has given us the weapons we need to defeat the devil. We know that the enemy cannot stand it when we get in the Word. We know that he cannot stand it when we fast and pray and lay ourselves out before the Lord. We just have to aim our God-given weapons at the enemy in the place where it hurts the most.

After David killed Goliath, David came to have a very close friendship with Jonathan, the son of King Saul. It was a relationship in which Jonathan was closer than a brother to David. As 1 Samuel 18:3 says, it was a covenant relationship in which Jonathan loved David "as his own soul." While this was happening, Saul became an enemy to David. He heard the women say, "Saul hath slain his thousands, and David his ten thousands" (1 Sam. 18:7), and jealousy of David's popularity overcame him. Saul recognized the potential for David to attain the position of king, and he determined in his heart that he would kill David.

One day, as David was playing his harp for Saul, the king took a javelin and threw it at David. He tried to kill the shepherd boy who had come to show love and kindness to him. As a result, David started to run and hid from Saul. The king may have had all the resources of the kingdom at his disposal, but he was unsuccessful in his mission because the Lord was with David.

David had to dwell in caves and hide like a criminal. And as he did, he began to write psalms that expressed his cry for deliverance from his enemies: "Deliver me from mine enemies, O my God: defend me from them that rise up against me" (Ps. 59:1). "Lord, you are going to have to fight my battles," David said. He did not take matters into his own hands, even though he wanted to in some cases. For instance, David had the opportunity to kill Saul a couple of times. Yet, he understood that vengeance belongs to God. He will repay our enemies. It is not for us to take matters into our own hands, but it is for us to pray for our enemies and allow the Lord to do what He needs to do in them.

In 1 Samuel 27, David went to Achish, the Philistine king of Gath, and raided some of the enemies of the Philistines. Even though he served the cause of the Philistines, someone betrayed him and told King Saul that he had gone to be with Achish. David wrote about this response of godless people in Psalm 53:1: "The fool hath said in his heart, There is no God. Corrupt are they, and have done abominable iniquity: there is none that doeth good."

While David was staying in the Philistine camp, he almost got comfortable. However, God did not want him to remain there because He had something for him to do. He had a kingdom—the nation of Israel—for him to run. First God moved the Philistine leaders to send David away from them because they were preparing to fight against Israel. They did not trust David to be true to them in the approaching battle. In addition, God allowed a serious problem to enter David's life so that he would seek Him. The Amalekites invaded Ziklag, when the wives and children of David and his men were staying alone there and took all of them captive.

Because of this desperate situation, the people wanted to kill David. Yet, in the midst of his great distress, "David encouraged himself in the LORD his God" (1 Sam. 30:6). Sometimes we can look to others for encouragement and help. But other times, no one is around to care for us. No one else understands the hurt and pain we feel. When the enemy wants to destroy us and all seems hopeless, that is the time we must encourage ourselves in God.

Being the man of God he knew he was called to be, David asked Abiathar the priest for the linen ephod. It was as if he were saying, "Lord, I know you have something for me to do, and I cannot run from it any longer. Lord, I have to step back into the role I know I was called to fulfill." As he began to step back into what God had for him, David prayed and asked God if he should pursue the Amalekites. God graciously, wonderfully restored all the wives and children to David and his men, who also recovered all the material goods that had been taken.

These are some of the highlights David must have remembered as he worshiped God the day he led the procession that brought the ark of the covenant to Jerusalem. He remembered how merciful the Lord had been to him, and he worshiped God with reckless abandon. We, too, must learn to worship God with the same wholeheartedness that David had. We must do it not just within the walls of a church building, but we must also go outside those walls to live among the people God has placed in our lives. Our worship to God is all about people coming to Christ. It is all about another person knowing the Christ who lives inside of you and me.

Worship is not about carrying a big Bible or a big cross. It is being kind to the person who does not have anything, the one who may smell a little bit, may have drunk some alcohol, or may be on drugs. Worship is taking the time to say, "I love you and God loves you." We must not turn our back on the unlovely, but we must instead be kind to people who are less fortunate. That is how you worship Him. That is how we serve Him.

The Relationship of Repentance and Worship

We learn more about David's wholehearted worship six chapters after he and the elders of Israel brought the ark of the covenant to Jerusalem. This was the time when "Satan stood up against Israel, and provoked David to number Israel" (1 Chron. 21:1). When David directed Joab, the commander of the army, to take the census, Joab replied, "Why would you do this and sin against the Lord?" However, because David persisted, Joab obeyed the king's command. How often do we follow in David's steps and continue to do what we know is not right, even when another servant of God warns us against it?

When Joab returned to David with the results of the census, he reported the sum of the number of the people as a thousand, thousand—a million—and an hundred thousand, a total of 1,100,000. Verse 7 records that God was displeased with what David had done, and in 1 Chronicles 21:10, He sent Gad, the seer, to offer him three choices of how he would like to receive God's judgment: either three years' famine, three months of being destroyed by their enemies, or three days under the sword of the Lord. Although David cried out to God to receive forgiveness, there was no option to escape the coming judgment.

God could have judged Israel any way He wanted, but He loved David so much that He gave him a choice. David wisely chose to "fall now into the hand of the LORD; for very great are his mercies" (1 Chron. 21:13). He said, "I know God is merciful, and I am going to count on His mercy." God sent an angel to Jerusalem "to destroy it: and as he was destroying, the LORD beheld, and he repented him of the evil" (v. 15). David's understanding of God was true. God was indeed very merciful to David and to His chosen people. He changed His mind and stopped the destruction of Jerusalem.

The angel of the Lord directed Gad to tell David to go to the threshing floor of Araunah and build an altar to the Lord there. With a repentant heart and in obedience to God's Word, David went to purchase the site of the threshing floor from Araunah. Even though Araunah said David could just have the place, David insisted on paying for it. "I will surely buy it of thee at a price," he said, "neither will I offer burnt offerings unto the LORD my God of that which doth cost me nothing" (2 Sam. 24:24). David said that he wouldn't dare to give the Lord something that cost him nothing. He paid Araunah six hundred shekels for it and sacrificed burnt offerings and peace offerings there. Because David offered this act of worship to God with humility and repentance, God commanded the angel to put his sword into its sheath and stop the destruction of Jerusalem. By this example of wholehearted worship, he modeled the way we are to live.

We must freely give of ourselves to God in fasting and prayer and in an upright walk and holy living. To give sacrificially in worship to God places us under His gracious mercy and care.

21

THE FRUIT OF FASTING

As I monitor my days of fasting, many changes occur. What is happening to me? I feel disoriented, like something is trying to overtake my mind, my understanding. Spirits have tried to occupy my body through many avenues, but they cannot fully gain an entrance. I have bound, rebuked, and prayed, but someone that I prayed for in the last week has left a deposit that I didn't ask for. I fasted three days last week and won many victories, but today I am struggling. I am not sleeping well at night, and I wake up frequently to pray. I feel tired, exhausted. Yet, there are things that make me happy; therefore I know I am not truly depressed.

The Lord told me to begin my fast yesterday, on Monday, and I made it only until five o'clock. Today is Tuesday, and I believe I should have continued it. I am going to do my best to make it the next three days. I ate about six doughnuts last night, and sugar always leads me to a place I really don't want to go. It acts as a depressant and pork does too. I know the Lord is calling me to a higher spiritual level, but my flesh wants to drag and not go there. I really need to consecrate and spend some quality time with the Lord, one-on-one.

Today is the beginning of the rest of my life. I am desperate and determined to gain total victory and deliverance in this temple—my body. I really am not concerned about title or position or even the approval of any man or woman now. I just need the Lord of lords and the King of kings to come into my heart and my soul and do the impossible, to move the immovable and to speak peace and joy to my soul. Only He can do that, you know. Only He, the One who died for us all, can do it.

Dear Lord, help me, for my soul longeth for You and the peace that I can only receive from You. You and only You can bring the deliverance I am seeking for this day and this hour. Lord, forgive my sins, the ones I know of and even those I know not of. Lord, I have no time for shame about what people may say or think. I just want to feel You the way I know only You can make me feel. I have never been embraced by any love like Your love. No food or drink has ever given me the delight that You bring.

Lord, I petition You with all my might, soul, and strength deliver me this day, for I know all power in heaven and Earth is given unto You. I know that You are all-powerful, all-knowing, and in all places at all times. Therefore, Lord, I totally submit my will to Your will and my thoughts to Your thoughts. I desire Your presence in my life in a strong and consistent way. I will be faithful to You and will do my best to love You and honor You from this day forward, for better or for worse until death do us part. Yes, I will be married to You. Even if I have a natural husband, You will always be my first love. Don't leave me in the bowels of hell, but, Lord, allow me to feast once again under Your shadow. I love You, Lord.

The Consequence of Disobeying God

The above instance is the second time I have experienced a sense of spiritual disorientation in the past twenty-plus years. The first time, which was worse, happened this way. A lady I knew in Iowa City, Iowa, was extremely depressed and full of darkness, living in an adulterous state. I felt that because she was nice to me she should be delivered. I—yes, I said *I* wanted her to be delivered completely. Even back then, when I was a young person, the Lord had done many miraculous acts through me. In this situation, God told me not to put my hands on this woman. However, I thought that since the Lord had given me prophetic words and used me to minister healing and deliverance to others, it was all right.

I was young and had zeal, but not according to knowledge. I had no one to teach me. The pastor's wife said she had only read about the gifts the Lord had given me. The pastor said he had absolutely no knowledge of the gifts of the Spirit. They said, "Everything you have said has been true and has come true, even those things people hadn't told anyone; the Lord has revealed it to you." People were afraid to be around me because I knew all about people instantly, even though I had not seen them before. I later discovered this was discernment. I was in the wrong place and didn't know it because you can go no higher than your leader and he had admitted that he had no knowledge.

When I laid hands on this girl, all the darkness, depression, and feelings of her past hurt transferred to me. Was I in sin? No! Was I prayed up? Yes! But, I, being young and lacking in knowledge, willfully disobeyed the Lord. I thought He would understand how I felt and would change His mind and be happy with my—and I do say *my*—decision. Well, God was so displeased with me, and I felt so bad. This was a change for me because I had always been a happy person since I was a little girl. I don't remember really feeling sad or down. I was always so friendly, loving, and kind to everyone I met.

The Lord spoke to me and said, "You will go through difficulty for three days, but after those three days you will be restored to normal without trace or residue of what occurred." This came true, just as the Lord had said. As a result, I have gone all over the world warning people about the transfer of spirits, how spirits will attack you and your mind, and the importance of being prayed up.

I have guarded my salvation, and never in twenty-one years have I committed adultery, fornication, or anything that any Christian would say has tempted them! I did disobey God when I should have fasted for twenty-four hours and only did it for twelve. Lack of temperance and self-control in eating—gluttony—caused this. It was my fault and no one else's.

This didn't just start with me. It began as a generational pattern when I would watch my mother sit and eat piles of food until it was all gone. As a little girl, I began to eat when I was happy, when I was sad, and just for the sake of eating. I remember that even when I was full I would always find room for more until I had to at times do push-ups before I could walk and leave the kitchen. Although I didn't really understand fasting, there were times I didn't eat anything and quickly lost weight, only to quickly gain it back.

Since I have received salvation through Christ, I have learned moderation but still need to work on self-control in eating. I love to cook, and I love to eat. Sometimes I have found myself eating after a counseling session, or I have gotten an urge to eat something while I am on the phone. It is usually not something healthy like a carrot or celery stick, but a sandwich, ice cream, or candy.

The devil is so slick and cunning in the devices he uses against us. If he can't get us to do those things that are well-recognized as evil, he tempts us through a side door, like overindulging in things like food, which is necessary, and ministry activities, which are good. He can speak to us so smoothly, just like he did in the Garden of Eden when he deceived Eve and sin came into our lives. We must expose the devil today and declare victory today and forevermore.

Three Days That Changed My Husband and Me

Three days seems like such a short time to change the course of history, but the Lord has done it before. For me, it was more than twenty years ago after three days of fasting, prayer, and consecration. I had been married about two years and had gone through the worst nightmare of my life because my husband, who was raised in the church, refused to serve the Lord or have anything to do with Him. It was pure torture to go home and have a conversation with him. I used to try to stay at work or at church just so I wouldn't have to deal with the abusive language or little games he would play to try to upset me.

I prayed and prayed, and finally I cried, "Lord, save him,

even if You have to give him to someone else." I meant what I said.

The Lord had mercy on me, and as I sat praying, crying, and pouring my heart out to Him, He told me, "Give me three days of fasting and prayer. Cut the television off. Say as few words as possible at work. On your break and lunch give that time to Me, talking to Me, submitting totally to My will and My way. When you wake in the morning, give the situation to Me; and when you come home from work, give it to me; and finally, at night before you go to bed, give it to Me."

I did exactly what the Lord said; I neither ate nor drank except to brush my teeth and to keep my breath fresh with mouthwash. I remained in place, expecting the Lord to take my husband from me since he didn't even come home during my fast. Although he had not done it before, he stayed at his workplace in the sleeping quarters it provided. I knew it was the Lord keeping him away while I completed my assignment of a three-day fast.

The first day of the fast was filled with apprehension because I thought that people would think of me as a failure. The second day I didn't care; I just wanted peace in my life. And the third day, he came home. I thought he would pack all his stuff and just leave, but he didn't. We talked, and I told him, "You know who God is, and you are fighting Him, not me." As we spoke, I further said, "We can't make it without the Lord."

For once, he agreed. He shared how his father was a preacher and that the people had treated him so badly that he never wanted to experience that. Then, for the first time, he admitted, "The Lord has called me to preach but I don't want to do it." I already knew this. When he didn't know I was listening I would hear him preaching to himself. As we continued to talk, I told him, "We are having a revival at the church. Why don't you come?" He agreed to come and hear our guest evangelist from Chicago.

My husband had never been to church with me since we had moved to Iowa two long years before. He went to church that night, and he was asked to sing because the pastor's wife remembered that I had told her he had a beautiful voice. He got up to sing and preached the message. The people were so thrilled that they asked him to sing again the next night, and he preached again. On the third night, he did the same thing.

The evangelist, who was very patient and kind, had a wonderful sense of discernment. "Brother," he told my husband, "when are you going to give up and accept your calling?" That is exactly what he did that night, and he has been preaching for about twenty years now. Just as God miraculously saved the Jews from being destroyed in the Persian Empire after Queen Esther's three-day fast, the Lord miraculously moved upon my husband to enter the calling He had for him after my three-day fast.

Focused on Christ; Submitting to Him

> Now, I am on another three-day fast. The first full day of fasting I felt so much clearer, and I realized how tired I was from trying to pray for others and pushing myself when I should have been in a resting state. I had just spent a week out of town at a conference on spiritual renewal and had then returned home to a week-long

meeting at church. I taught on Wednesday night and was tired but refused none who came in for counseling or prayer. All were healed, helped, inspired, and delivered, but it left me exhausted. The devil launched a full attack on my spirit.

Today I only feel a trace of the weariness and confusion that was there at the beginning of my fast. I closed the door and just prayed to the Lord and focused on Him. I repented of all sins and submitted my righteousness to the righteousness of Christ. I thank Him for a mind to pray and a mind to live right, a mind to submit. Some people can't think for themselves or pray for themselves when the enemy attacks them. However, I know this is just a stepping-stone to take me higher in the Lord.

The second day, the Lord showed me myself and what I needed to correct. He had instructed me to do some things, but I didn't hear Him clearly because I was full of what I wanted. I had my own agenda. Now, however, it is His way or no way. I don't want it like Burger King; I want it the King's way. I listened to the Lord's instructions, obeyed them, and amazingly enough, I am clear as a bell, with no trace of any problems. Temperance is in place, clarity is a definite, and I am connected to God. I am able to serve the Lord and follow His instructions. I had become so busy with His business that I left Him out.

Appendix A

A SUPPLEMENT ON STRESS

CHAPTER 11 INTRODUCED us to problems related to stress and remedies that can help provide relief. However, much more can be said, and the purpose of this appendix is to provide additional information. As we begin to learn more about stress, we recognize that there are three different types: systemic or physiological, psychological, and social. Systemic stress is related to the tissue system. Psychological stress is associated with cognitive factors leading to the evaluation of threat, and, of course, social stress comes from the disruption of a social unit or a system. In any terms, stress is simply confusion.[1]

According to a 1990 study by Davidson and Neal, it is believed that all illness is in part stress-related. Looking at the schematic charts, stress produces a cycle in which the dynamic conflict of personality characteristics leads to diagnosis and treatment and possibly death. The dynamic conflict of personality characteristics could lead to psychological consequences—depression, anger, and denial—which lead to a problem with the endocrine system, the production of glucose, or transient or nontransient diabetes. The cycle of psychological consequences could lead to immune surveillance or immune suppression, which progresses to tumor formation and could possibly lead to cancer or worse.[2]

When stress comes and is persistent and continual, the configuration of one cell changes. As this cell and others like it grow, they multiply and continue to multiply, according to Drs. Stanley Robbins and Ramzi Cotran. Because they are irregular, these tumor cells grow faster than the other cells until one ends up with a neoplasm. If this is not stopped, it will continue to grow out of control until it turns into a cancer, which is essentially just a rotten piece of tissue that is nonfunctional and has to be removed. The occurrence of cancer may happen at any of various sites, including the breast, the pancreas, the liver, the ovaries, and the stomach.[3]

One out of four people will develop some type of cancer, some due to genetics, which would put them at greater risk. It is estimated that most cancers are the result of unhealthy lifestyles or are significantly contributed to by things such as smoking, alcohol, unhealthy diet, certain sexual behaviors, and ultraviolet light. Personalities and emotional factors have also been implicated. The internalization of anger and aggression and the suppression of emotions play a significant role. Stressful life events, high levels of depression and anxiety, and denial are among the culprits.

Stress can be very damaging. Dr. Steven Applebaum suggests that stress on people with Type-A personalities will cause coronary artery disease.[4] And Dr. James B. Wyngaarden and others warn about the elevation of blood pressure and the arteries not being able to expand or have the elasticity they should.[5] If an artery ruptures in the heart, the result is a heart attack, a cardiovascular accident. If an artery ruptures in the brain, it is called a stroke, a cerebrovascular accident.

When one has a heart attack, the tissue will probably break where the artery breaks. The heart will become nonfunctional at that point; tissue dies unless collateral or extra circulation is formed there. If the heart becomes nonfunctional, it does not beat the way it should. While it would regularly beat like a pump, it now beats like half of a pump and fails to provide an adequate amount of blood for the tissues in the body, Congestive heart failure, a buildup of fluid in and around the heart, may cause swelling in the feet and extreme weariness from walking just a short distance. If the malfunction of the heart is really severe, one could die because the heart is nonfunctional.

Drs. Meyer Friedman and Ray Rosenman have been credited with the most famous attempt to relate stress to heart disease. They described the Type-A and Type-B personalities, and presented the advanced thought that the Type-A personality was an independent risk factor for the development of coronary artery disease. Type-A people cannot rest or relax without feeling guilty about not doing something. They tend to have constant challenges and competitive attitudes, even when they are nonexistent. They are not able to be flexible but are instead rigid in their pursuit of any achievement. Type-A people tend to have several lines of thought at the same time as they rush through meals and constantly interrupt others. Most fail to have satisfying relationships because they are self-centered and preoccupied with their own plans and purposes. Type-B people, on the other hand, have less sense of urgency about their work. Therefore, they relax and have less risk for coronary artery disease.[6]

Applebaum has shown that stress, in addition to causing coronary artery disease, may also lead to alienation, hostility, family problems, marital problems, alcohol and drug use, and possibly suicide.[7] If it is not dealt with properly, anxiety and stress can be very costly to all people in all situations. It causes many diseases and affects just about every organ system. Even the American Medical Association now agrees that stress is causative or related to disease processes.[8]

Finding Relief and Receiving Healing

Dr. Herbert Benson of Harvard Medical School defines stress as "environmental conditions requiring behavioral adjustment." This thought is similar to the original medical concept that was conceived by Dr. Hans Selye in the 1950s, which essentially viewed stress as a reaction to the situation that causes the stress, rather than the physical, human, psychological or psychosocial condition.[9] He believed that disease could very well be related to continual stress.

Stress can, indeed, cause disease. Some may say, "Oh, it is just stress. I have just lost some hair. I am not eating. I am depressed." However, a very real result of stress is that hormonal changes occur during stress and may even cause a lactating mother, a mother who is giving milk to her baby, to completely stop producing milk. Also if a woman is still having menstrual cycles, her menses may decrease or stop, or it may increase.

Other illnesses that may develop from stress and anxiety, especially in children, are stomachaches, headaches, and even a psychosis that causes blindness, as Drs. Jan van Dijk and Catherine Nelson suggest.[10] Many children who have been trained and have stopped bed-wetting will regress to bed-wetting when a stressful situation comes. Yes, stress can affect people of all ages, from children to adults. It is very important that neither our children nor adults suffer continual stress.

Billions of dollars are spent on stress management each year. A few things that tend to help relieve stress are time management, proper nutrition, exercise, finding alternatives to frustration, setting goals, and taking action to stop smoking and drinking. Each person must find a way to relieve his pent-up energy and frustration without causing conflicts with his fellow man. This, essentially, assures peace of mind and also earns the goodwill, respect, and even the love of one's neighbors. To attain this highest degree of security and most noble status symbol is to achieve what the Bible teaches: "Do unto others as you would have them do unto you."

It is so important that we learn how to relax and not allow stress and anxiety to overwhelm us. We must not allow offenses to cause us to be anxious or disturbed. We must realize that the cause and the effect of the stressor is too great to entertain for long. Whatever our stress is, we must quickly find some type of relief that will keep it from affecting our bodies and our minds.

One man had a life-threatening disease that he believed was due to stress. He alleviated the stress, took vitamin C, and had a total recovery, with an extension of his life. Another man had suffered so many insults from people he loved that the stress had caused a very large cancer to develop in his stomach. But after he prayed and gave the situation and its stress to the Lord, the cancer was miraculously reduced to the size of a pinpoint when the operation came. God was, indeed, gracious to heal, because cancer does not usually regress.

In a final story about God's care for problems related to stress, a believer who loved the Lord fell and broke her foot one day as she was busy doing a lot of things for ministry. She was also diabetic, and this meant she would heal more slowly than other people and would probably have to be in a cast for some time. When she went to the emergency room, a body of believers began to pray for her. As a result, all the pain left her foot while she was meeting with the orthopedic surgeon, who had the set of X-rays that confirmed the break. With the cessation of pain, follow-up X-rays showed no fracture, and the surgeon told her, "This is a documented miracle."

Appendix B

ANOREXIA NERVOSA, BULIMIA, AND OVEREATING

CHAPTER 11 IDENTIFIED harmful eating patterns as a kind of problem that may result from stress in a person's life. One of these destructive eating patterns is anorexia nervosa, which led to the death of the famed music star Karen Carpenter. Anorexia is "an eating disorder primarily affecting adolescent girls and young women, characterized by pathological fear of becoming fat, distorted body image, excessive dieting, and emaciation." Bulimia may be defined as "a habitual disturbance in eating behavior mostly affecting young women of normal weight characterized by frequent episodes of grossly excessive food intake followed by self-induced vomiting to avert weight gain."

Karen and her brother Richard both started their careers very young and were driven by a desire to prove that they were someone, to be at the top. Though they had many failures, they provided the kind of music many people wanted to hear and climbed the ladder of success. They sold millions of records and released many hits, including "We Have Only Just Begun." However, the pressure of stardom, the pressure of feeling that you are not good enough, caused both of them to have serious problems related to stress.

When Karen thought about herself, she felt that she was never small enough. She struggled with anorexia until the 1970s, when she weighed less than one hundred pounds and took laxatives daily. By the 1980s she had heart failure and died at age 32. Richard, on the other hand, began taking sleeping pills in 1970, and because of the effects of this problem, he was unable to play by 1978. He eventually went into rehab in 1990.[1]

Bulimia, another harmful eating pattern, caused much suffering for another young woman. Even though she could not be considered overweight, her peers told her that she was ugly because she was a little bit hippy. As a result, she decided that she was going to lose weight in an unhealthy way. She would eat and then run into the bathroom and force herself to vomit. This young woman, very attractive with her beautiful, long, flowing blonde-brown hair and creamy skin, began to seek the admiration of boys. She would sneak out of the house to go to parties when she was fourteen years old, and one night she went to a party and began to drink. Before she knew what was happening, she had sex with three boys and did not remember anything about it until someone told her the next day.

She was devastated and fell into a vicious cycle of anger and depression—and eating and vomiting. She was in a bulimic state for approximately three years, until she finally decided she should give the Lord a try. He completely delivered her from bulimia and low self-esteem, and she stuck with Him. She learned that He would never fail her.

Millions of people respond to stress by the harmful eating pattern we know as overeating. People eat while they talk on the phone and reach for something to munch on when they hear something disturbing. People eat when they are sad, disappointed, depressed, or bored. They feel guilty after they eat too much, and as they continue to overeat, they feel like it is no use to try to get out of the addictive cycle of guilt, remorse, more eating, depression, and an increase in weight. Many stop exercising, and if there is no intervention, they become obese. The more weight they gain, the worse they feel.

Some people have a sugar addiction that leads to binge eating, perhaps for a weekend or for weeks at a time. Fats in many foods will evoke a desire for sugar and cause one to engage in uncontrollable eating. A person with sugar addiction must totally avoid sugar for a period of time until there is no longer a craving for sweets. At that point, it is important that one does not even taste sweets. Many say a little won't hurt but it does when there is an addiction such as sugar, drugs, or alcohol.

How, then, can we stop the terrible cycle of addiction that takes the form of overeating? We must allow offenses and stress to be stepping-stones to strength rather than defeat. We must open our spirit to Christ and release our struggles and needs to Him. He will provide deliverance and healing for any and all eating problems we may have.

Appendix C

A TEENAGER'S THOUGHTS ON PREJUDICE AND STRESS

CHAPTER 6 WARNED against the spirit of negativity and noted that the spirit of hatred can be reflected in the form of prejudice, which grows from one person feeling that he is better than another person. Chapter 11 described the spirit of stress as a very destructive force, a source of many struggles in our lives. The following essays, written by Gwendolyn Rodgers while she was attending Brookstone High School, represent the thoughts of a teenager on prejudice, the stress of peer pressure, and the negativity that can follow the stress of "sweating the small stuff." I believe her words provide great insight for us.

PREJUDICE: JUST A ZEBRA

Zebras are beautiful, horse-like animals that happen to be black and white. When we refer to a zebra, we don't ask, Which part is it, the black part or the white part? We just call it a zebra. So why are people different? Why is the human race is divided into subgroups?

Friends have told me that they don't see me as black, but just as me. I understand what they mean, but some people of all races fail to realize that being called black isn't an insult. While I was working at camp this summer, one of the counselors told me that I'm "not that black." I asked her if her statement was supposed to be a compliment, and she said yes.

I think she noticed that I took offense at her comment, so she tried to dig herself out. She told me that I don't "talk black" or "act black." I explained to her that being black doesn't mean speaking broken English, wearing hair extensions down to my toes, or living in the projects. Stereotyping all blacks the way she did is like assuming that all Chinese are excellent math students or all blondes are airheads. I felt that she looked at me as if I were a "good black," or nothing more than a dog that had gone through training school.

Many people are oblivious to their little expressions of prejudice. One day while I was sitting on the floor by my locker, someone stepped over me and placed her hand on my head. As she walked away, I noticed that she wiped her hand on her jeans, as if to imply that my hair was dirty. At first I was highly offended, but there was nothing I could do.

Another time, in my freshman year, I was walking in the hall and accidentally brushed against a senior. She moved away in disgust and looked at her sleeves as if some of my "color" had stained her (million-dollar) blouse. I couldn't figure it out. If she couldn't bear the thought of my brown skin touching her shirt, why does she run to lie out on the beach or go to the tanning bed everyday? I understand that this may be the twenty-first century, but some people still have the mentality of the nineteenth-century slave owners; they feel they are better than blacks.

Thinking about these incidents made me wonder how the other blacks in the upper [high] school feel about being a minority. Ashleigh (eleventh grade) says, "Sometimes it feels kind of weird; sometimes I can't relate [to other students here]." I wondered if attending Brookstone longer would alter the answer, so I asked Jon (twelfth grade). He said that he doesn't really think about it. Next I asked Marcus (tenth grade) how it feels to be one of the few blacks at school. "Well, this is a predominantly white school," he answered, "so you have to deal with it."

After being in the Brookstone school system for twelve years, I can say that the whole race issue isn't something that constantly tugs at my mind. I have really great friends who notice my skin color but look through it to see who I am and not what color I am.

In conclusion, try not to treat people any worse than you would treat yourself. Treating someone better with good intentions is just as bad as treating them poorly with bad intentions. Both kinds of actions are signals that a person is somehow different. And remember, don't separate the colors; it's just a zebra.

Peer Pressure: Rock or Clay?

Do you ever wonder why we do certain things and why we do those certain things in a specific way? People today, especially in our generation, have been molded and shaped by society. If you are clay, you are easily influenced, and you may "jump off bridges" just because everyone else does. If you are a rock, you are deeply rooted and do what you want, what makes you happy. Unfortunately, even a rock is eventually reshaped and smoothed by the river's current, or it is broken over time. So which are you, rock or clay?

The flawless faces on the billboards, the gap-less smiles on magazines, and the perfect bodies on television all influence our lives and, without giving us a reason, tell us how we are supposed to look, act, and feel. Who are the people who determine whether something is wrong or right, sane or insane, cool or nerdy? Why do we allow those people to separate us? I believe that those "unnamed" individuals are the ones who have the biggest mouths and therefore set the rules, and leave them for us to follow.

Does dressing differently or changing yourself externally make you an individual, or are you just like all the other individuals who make it a task to be different? Of course we are all different, but our upbringing and the morals and environments we have been exposed to are all very similar. So when we decide that something is cool or uncool, is it society talking, or do we all actually feel that way?

North Face, Steve Madden, Birkenstock, New Balance, Timberland, Nine West, Jansport, Saucony, and Adidas are just a few name-brand items that have "marked" Brookstone students for years. In the beginning, I'm sure one person wore something and everyone else joined in because it was a fad. Eventually, however, people stopped purchasing for pleasure and started buying from pressure. I've noticed that every clique has a specific style. In other words, the students who hang together here dress alike. Is this because they like what they are buying and wearing, or is it because they feel that it will make them more acceptable?

As we have all noticed, Jacob dresses like no other student here in the Upper School. I asked him why he chooses to dress in such a unique manner, and he told me it makes him happy. Then I asked him if going out of your way to be different is the same as going out of your way to get the newest fashion, and he said, "Absolutely."

Next, I asked Kelsey (ninth grade) why she chooses to make her own unique fashion statements, and she said, "It's because I am different." My response was that we are all different internally, so why choose to do so externally as well? Then she explained that her dress is a form of expression. Caroline, a senior, agreed with Kelsey and added, "I think any choice you make in life expresses who you are in some way."

So I wonder, when one wears a North Face jacket, is he saying, "Look at me, I ski!" or "Look at me, I want to be accepted"? When I asked twenty-five students if they owned any North Face gear (jacket, backpack, shoes, or fleece), twenty said "yes," and only four of the twenty actually ski. To be brutally honest, I asked my mother to buy a North Face jacket for me because I thought it was cool and strange because of the random pockets. I wore my beloved (not to mention expensive) jacket with pride and was disappointed to find that it couldn't keep a fire warm if it had to. Could yours?

So, honestly ask yourself, "Am I a rock? Or a lump of clay?" Don't be different because it's cool or because you are to do so. Find who you are and what makes you happy, even if it means being the same as some other people.

Negativity and Stress: Sweating the Small Stuff

"Oh, Becky! Look at that girl's belt! It like totally doesn't match her shoes! If I were her, I'd just die!" As idiotic as these statements seem, they are very realistic, and we often hear them. Some of us stress over issues that aren't worth a bowl of stew: split ends, matching accessories, or dates for homecoming. How many times do you find yourself fretting over something that really doesn't matter? And then what do you do? You go around to everyone and bore them to death with your so-called problem.

Although the thought of someone else's hair in your food is really gross, is it worth ranting and raving about? I've been out with people who go overboard when something is wrong with their meals. Telling the manager and getting something new to eat is one thing, but going on and on about the "mishap" and spoiling everyone else's dinner is another. Some of us complain about things that we are actually lucky to have.

Once, while chatting with a couple friends in the hall, I overheard someone say, "My mom only gave me two hundred dollars this month!" By merely reading this statement, one would suppose that the student was bragging. But, oh, no, she wasn't. In fact, this certain someone had the audacity to complain about receiving more than a person on minimum wage makes in about two weeks.

Here at Brookstone, we complain about broken machines, cold air, and the need for more eating time. Although these issues need addressing, do we ever take time to look at the good things that Brookstone has given us, things like ten-year friendships and superior education?

Last summer I was lucky enough to visit Nigeria, in western Africa, for a month. While I was in the poorer section of the area, I watched little children chase a skinny old rooster. They laughed and played, even though they had little or no money, and they were happy. They didn't know they were poor because they were never informed. When I returned to America and went to Wendy's, a child yelled at his mother, "I said I wanted chicken nuggets!" I was amazed at how spoiled the child was and at how much we take for granted.

Of course, everyone sweats some small stuff, but don't let trivial issues consume your mind. Whenever something goes wrong, find some good in it, even though it may be difficult. Don't fail to realize how truly blessed you are, and don't waste life by mumbling and complaining.

The next time you're stressed about something like a bad haircut, ask yourself, "Hey, why am I sweating the small stuff?"

ABOUT THE AUTHOR

DR. GLORIA JOHNSON-RODGERS is a family practice physician, humanitarian, and author who began life in a shotgun house with a room off the side in a small town called Shaw, Mississippi. She grew up on commodity food and a lot of love. She decided to become a physician at the age of five after watching a man die because of the lack of adequate medical care. Dr. Rodgers has always loved to help those who are unable to care for themselves. Even as a child she would cook, clean, and care for the elderly in her community.

For over two decades Dr. Rodgers has empowered the young and the old in her local community, serving over sixty thousand individuals in one year through clothing, food, and counseling. The facility from which she serves the community is the Toys for Tots center for the area; it also serves as an adult day health center and provides childcare and pre-school services with high merits from the state.

For her servanthood abroad, Dr. Rodgers has received numerous awards, including the Marion Merrill Dow Humanitarian Award; the Bola Immaculate Humanitarian

Award of Excellence, Nigeria, West Africa; the Legislative Black Caucus Volunteer of the Year Award, Atlanta, Georgia; the Mason Theological Seminary Award for Foreign Service; Voices from Lane Bryant and Charming; National Sojourner Truth Meritorious Service Award; President's Bush Daily Points of Light Award, Washington, D.C.; National Caring Award, Washington, D.C., in honor of Mother Teresa; and many others.

Millions of children in Nigeria, West Africa, are yearly deprived of the simple things in life, such as proper food, clothing, good drinking water, health care, and schools. The problem is poverty. Cross River, Rivers, Anambra , Delta, Kogi, Imo, Edo, Oyo, Benue, Engu, Lagos, Taraba, and Abia states, not to mention villages all over Nigeria, have been positively affected in a tangible way by Dr. Rodgers's work. She has also made an impact through monies, food, healthcare teams, and health supplies in the following countries: Haiti, the Dominican Republic, England, Brazil, and South Africa.

Dr. Rodgers has been blessed with an impeccable professional career and received numerous awards. However, her first love, the elderly and children, has brought her full circle, and now she is doing what she enjoys most—providing care to those who can by no other means support themselves through the Gwendolyn Wilkes Rainbow Center and Eagles Landing Academy Centers and Schools International, which are multifaceted nonprofit organizations. In 2003, Dr. Rodgers fulfilled one of her dreams and wrote her first book, *Author of Offense*. In addition, she has cowritten three other publications. Although Dr. Rodgers's accomplishments are many, her most cherished accomplishment is her love, dedication, and devotion to her husband, Superintendent (Dr.) Charles Rodgers; their four children, Gwendolyn, Charles "Chip" Jr., Elizabeth Megan, Adam James; and her church and community family.

BIBLIOGRAPHY

Anthon, Catherine Parker, et al. *Textbook of Anatomy and Physiology*. St. Louis, MO: The C. V. Mosby Company, 1979. pp. 668–675.

Applebaun, Steven. *Stress Management for Healthcare Professionals*. Rockville, MD: Aspen Publications, 1981. pp. 6, 36, 150, 153, 156, 168, 214, 216.

Banks, James and Barry Beyer, K. *The World Past and Present.* MacMillan/McGraw-Hill School Publishing Company, 1993. pp. 157 ("Idol Gods"), p. 264 ("Newton"), pp. 165–166 ("Alexander the Great").

Baun, Peter. *Alexander, the Great.* New York: McGraw-Hill Book Company, 1968.

Bean, Bobby. *This Is the Church of God in Christ*. Atlanta, GA: Underground Epics Publishing, 2001.

Behrman, Richard E., M.D.; Vaugh, Victor C. III, M.D. *Nelson Textbook of Pediatrics.* Philadelphia: W. B. Saunders Company, 1987. pp. 54–58.

Berne, Robert; Levy, Matthew N.; and Samuel, E. *Physiology.* Mosby, 1983. pp. 401–402, 751, 986–987, 1046–1047, 1066.

Berube, Margery. *Webster's II New College Dictionary.* Boston, MA: Houghton Mifflin Company, 1995.

The Carpenters: Harmony and Heartbreak. A & E Biography. 1998.

Boa, Kenneth, Ph.D. *The New Open Bible.* Thomas Nelson, Inc., 1990.

Cassidy, James, Jr. *Through Indian Eyes.* Pleasantville, NY: Readers Digest, 1995. pp. 149, 237, 241, 255, 371.

Church, Leslie, Ph.D. *Matthew Henry's Commentary.* Grand Rapids, MI: Zondervan Publishing House, 1961. pp. 1844–1845.

Clemmons, Itheil C. *Bishop C. H. Mason, and the Roots of the Church of God in Christ, Centennial Edition.* Bakersfield, CA: Pneuma Life Publishing, 1996.

Cohn, Peter F., Dr., and Cohn, Joan. *Heart Talk.* Boston, MA: Harcourt Brace Jovanovich Publishers, 1987. pp. 57–75.

Cole, Matthew. "Details." *American Gigolo,* June/July 2003. pp. 88–90.

Cunningham, Gary F., M.D.; MacDonald, Paul C., M.D.; and Gant, Norman F., M.D. *Williams Obstetrics.* Norwalk, CT: Appleton E. Lange. pp. 13; 77–78; "Extra Menses," p. 25.

Farr, Roger C., and Strickland, Dorothy. *Coast to Coast.* Orlando, FL: Harcourt Brace & Company, 1997. pp. 160–173.

Gibbon, Edward. *The Decline and Fall of the Roman Empire.* New York: Random House, Inc.

Grinnan, Edward. *Angels on Earth* (July/August 2000): 3–6.

Grinnan, Edward, *Angels on Earth* (March/April 2000): 24–25.

Grinnan, Edward, *Angels on Earth* (May/June 2000): 38–40.

Haffner, Craig, and Holloway, Kevin, dir. *Angels, the Mysterious Messengers.* Greystone, 1994.

Hart, Roger. *Witchcraft.* New York: G. P. Putnam's Sons, 1973.

Larvin, Asuncion. *Sexuality and Marriage in Colonial Latin America.* Lincoln, NE: University of Nebraska Press, 1992. pp. 178–191.

Masters, William H., and Johnson, Virginia. *Human Sexuality.* Boston, MA: Little, Brown and Company, 1985.

Messerli, Franz H., M.D. *The Heart and Hypertension.* New York: Yorke Medical Books, 1987. pp. 465–475.

Monat, Alan, and Lazarus, Richard. *Stress and Coping.* New York: Columbia University Press, 1991. pp. 2–3, 10, 34, 97.

Olsen, Ken. *Exorcism.* Nashville, TN: Thomas Nelson Publishers, 1992. p. 77.

Robbins, Stanley, M.D., and Cotran, Ramzi, S., M.D. *Pathologic Basis of Disease.* Philadelphia, PA: W. B. Saunders Company, 1979.

Russell, Jeffrey. *Witchcraft in the Middle Ages.* New York: Cornell University, 1972. pp. 1, 27, 167.

Scofield, D. D. *New Scofield Study Bible, Holy Bible.* New York: Oxford University Press, 1967.

"Dennis Nilsen." *Serial Killer/Sexual Predators.* Courtroom Television Network, LLC., 2003.

Shakespeare, William. *Macbeth.* New York: Washington Square Press, 1992. pp. 17–18.

Slaby, Andrew E., M.D., Ph.D., P.P.H., *Sixty Ways to Make Stress Work for You.* Atlanta, GA: Psychiatric Institute of Atlanta, 1988.

Soustelle, Jacques. *The Aztecs.* Stanford, CA: Stanford University Press, 1961. pp. 143–147.

Stern, Peter. *The Encyclopedia of World History.* Boston, MA: Houghton Mifflin Company, 2001. p. 71.

Synan, Vinson, H. *The Holiness-Pentecostal Movement in the United States.* Grand Rapids, MI: Wm. B. Eerdmans Publishing Company, 1971.

The Amplified Bible. Grand Rapids, MI: Zondervan Publishing House, 1987.

The New Encyclopedia Britannica. Chicago: Encyclopedia Britannica, Inc., 1994. p. 240.

Vander, Arthur, et al, *Human Physiology, the Mechanism of Body Function.* New York: McGraw-Hill Publishing Company, 1990.

Wyngaarden, James B., M.D., and Smith, Lloyd H., Jr., M.D. *Cecil Textbook of Medicine.* Philadelphia, PA: W. B. Saunders Company, 1982.

NOTES

CHAPTER 1

THE MINISTRY OF ANGELS

1. *Angels: Mysterious Messengers*, dir. Rex Hauck and Donna Lusitana, written by Craig Haffner (Greystone Television, 1994).

2. Ibid.

3. Ibid.

4. Itheil C. Clemmons, *Bishop C. H. Mason, and the Roots of the Church of God in Christ, Centennial Edition* (Bakersfield, CA: Pneuma Life Publishing, 1996).

5. Edward Grinnan, "My Conversation with the Trumpet Man," *Angels on Earth*, March 2000, Guidepost Publication (New York).

6. "Frederick Douglass Quotes," ThinkExist.com, http://thinkexist.com/quotation/without_a_struggle-there_can_be_no_progress/205797.html (accessed November 18, 2008).

CHAPTER 4

LUST

1. William H. Masters and Virginia Johnson, *Human Sexuality* (Boston, MA: Little, Brown, and Company, 1985).

2. William Shakespeare, *Macbeth* (New York: Washington Square Press, 1992), 17–18.

Chapter 5

Idolatry and Witchcraft

1. Jaques Soustelle, *The Aztecs* (Stanford, CA: Stanford University Press, 1961), 143–147; and Peter Stern, *The Encyclopedia of World History* (Boston, MA: Houghton Mifflin Co., 2001), 71.

2. Ibid.

3. Ibid.

4. Ibid.

5. Jeffrey Russell, *Witchcraft in the Middle Ages* (New York: Cornell University, 1972), 1, 27, 167.

6. Ibid.

7. Source needed.

8. Source needed.

9. Roger Hart, *Witchcraft* (New York: G. P. Putnam and Sons), 1973.

Chapter 7

Variance, Wrath, Strife, Sedition, and Heresies

1. Dr. Bobby Bean, *This Is the Church of God in Christ* (Atlanta, GA: Underground Epics Publishing, 2001).

Chapter 8

Emulations, Envyings, Murders

1. "A Tribute to Pete Maravich," Focus on the Family Daily Broadcast, November 12, 2008, http://listen.family.org/daily/A000001584.cfm (accessed November 18, 2008).

Chapter 9

Offenses

1. Martha Brockenbrough, "The Greatest Mistakes of All Time," MSN Encarta, http://encarta.msn.com/column_accidentalinventions_marthahome/the_greatest_mistakes_of_all_time.html (accessed November 18, 2008).

Chapter 11

Stress

1. Alan Monat and Richard Lazarus, *Stress and Coping* (New York: Columbia University Press, 1991), 2–3, 10, 34, 97.

2. Ibid.

Chapter 13

Death

1. Edward Grinnan, *Angels on Earth.*

Appendix A

A Supplement on Stress

1. Monat and Lazarus.

2. Ibid.

3. Drs. Stanley Robbins and Ramzi Cotran, *Pathologic Basis of Disease* (Philadelphia, PA: W. B. Saunders Co., 1979).

4. Dr. Steven Applebaum, *Stress Management for Healthcare Professionals* (Rockville, MD: Aspen Publications, 1981), 6, 36, 150, 153, 156, 168, 214, 216.

5. Drs. James B. Wyngaarden and Lloyd H. Smith Jr., *Cecil Textbook of Medicine* (Philadelphia, PA: W. B. Saunders Co., 1982).

6. Drs. Peter F. Cohn and Joan Cohn, *Heart Talk* (Boston, MA: Harcourt Brace Jovanovich Publishers, 1987), 57–75.

7. Applebaum.

8. Drs. Sheldon Cohen, Denise Janicki-Deverts, Gregory E. Miller, "Psychological Stress and Disease," Journal of the American Medical Association (298:1685–1687), October 10, 2007, http://jama.ama-assn.org/cgi/content/extract/298/14/1685 (accessed November 18, 2008).

9. "Stress (Psychology)," NationMaster.com, http://www.nationmaster.com/encyclopedia/Stress-(psychology) (accessed November 18, 2008).

10. David Brown and Elizabeth Bates, "A Personal View of Changes in Deaf-Blind Population, Philosophy, and Needs," Deaf-Blind Perspectives (Vol. 12, Issue 3), Spring 2005, ftp://ftp.tr.wou.edu/dbp/apr2005.txt (accessed November 18, 2008).

Appendix B

Anorexia Nervosa, Bulimia, and Overeating

1. *The Carpenters: Harmony and Heartbreak*, A & E Biography, Harmony and Heartbreak, 1998.

TO CONTACT THE AUTHOR

Dr. Gloria Johnson Rodgers

P.O. Box 1580

Columbus, GA 31902

GAJRODGERS@AOL.COM

(706) 320-9012